IOWA TRIVIA

REVISED EDITION

IOWA TRIVIA

REVISED EDITION

**COMPILED BY JANICE BECK STOCK,
ALAN BECK, AND KEN BECK**

Rutledge Hill Press®
Nashville, Tennessee

A Division of Thomas Nelson, Inc.
www.ThomasNelson.com

Published in Nashville, Tennessee, by Rutledge Hill Press®,
a Division of Thomas Nelson Publishers, Inc.,
P.O. Box 141000
Nashville, Tennessee 37214

Library of Congress Cataloging-in-Publication Data

Stock, Janice Beck, 1954–
    Iowa trivia / by Janice Beck, Alan Beck, and Ken Beck.—Rev. ed.
    p. cm.
    ISBN 1-55853-942-5
    1. Iowa—Miscellanea. I. Beck, Alan, 1956– II. Beck, Ken, 1951–
III. Title.
    F621.S84 2001
    977.7—dc21   2001048552

Printed in the United States of America.

01 02 03 04 05 — 5 4 3 2 1

PREFACE

This book was designed to be informative, interesting, and entertaining. We hope to give fellow Iowans a greater awareness of their state's rich heritage and continuing unique role. We also hope it will entice others to come visit and learn more about the Hawkeye State.

But whoever you are and wherever you're from, it is our wish that you have fun with this book and that it helps you realize the claim of the state's division of tourism has been proven true time and time again.

First question: In 2000, Iowa adopted what new state slogan?

Answer: Iowa—fields of opportunity.

To the wonderful people of
the state of Iowa

TABLE OF CONTENTS

GEOGRAPHY

C H A P T E R   O N E

Q. The state's geographic center is in what county?

A. Story County.

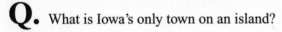

Q. For how many miles does the Des Moines River flow through Iowa?

A. 485.

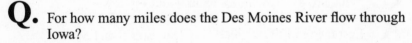

Q. What is Iowa's only town on an island?

A. Sabula.

Q. Where can one find Snake Alley, designated by *Ripley's Believe It or Not!* as the crookedest street in the world?

A. Burlington.

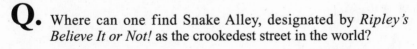

Q. What was the original name of Des Moines?

A. Fort Raccoon.

Q. The Nodaway, Middle Nodaway, and East Nodaway Rivers in southwest Iowa take their name from the Indian word for what reptile?

A. Rattlesnake.

Q. The name of what town in Clayton County honors a bedouin emir of Algeria?

A. Elkader.

Q. For whom was Oskaloosa named?

A. Chief Osceola's wife.

Q. What are the five largest natural lakes in Iowa?

A. East Okoboji, West Okoboji, Clear, Spirit, and Storm.

Q. What popular ice cream treat was invented in Onawa in 1920?

A. Eskimo Pie.

Q. How many counties are in Iowa?

A. Ninety-nine.

Q. What is Iowa's largest county by land area?

A. Kossuth (979 sq. mi.).

Q. What city is known both as "the Pearl of the Mississippi" and as "Melon City"?

A. Muscatine.

———◆———

Q. What is the only village in the Amana Colonies without the word Amana in it?

A. Homestead.

———◆———

Q. What two towns were named for the first letters of the names of six pretty women who accompanied railroad officials to the sites?

A. Le Mars and Delmar.

———◆———

Q. John I. Blair, builder of the Chicago and Northwestern and director of seventeen railroads, has what two towns in Iowa named for him?

A. Blairstown and Blairsburg.

———◆———

Q. What is Iowa's newest town?

A. Vedic City (incorporated in 2001 near Fairfield).

———◆———

Q. In the past, what was the greatest number of covered bridges at one time found in Madison County?

A. Nineteen.

———◆———

Q. Originally, what was the name of Atlantic supposed to be?

A. Pacific.

Q. What is the most common translation of the Indian word *Iowa*?

A. "Beautiful land."

Q. What northwest Iowa attraction was listed as a National Historic Landmark on February 23, 2001?

A. The Grotto of the Redemption, at West Bend.

Q. What two explorers met with the Missouri and Oto Indians at Council Bluffs in 1804?

A. Lewis and Clark.

Q. Living in McCausland until he was eight, Buffalo Bill Cody was born near what other Scott County town?

A. LeClaire.

Q. The state's first interurban concrete highway connected what two cities?

A. Clear Lake and Mason City.

Q. According to the 2000 Census, Des Moines, with a population of 198,682, ranked where on the list of national city populations?

A. Ninety-fifth (slipped from 81st in 1990).

Q. The state's smallest city park is situated in the middle of the road in what town?

A. Hiteman.

Q. Where is the Prairie's Edge Nature Center?

A. Vernon Springs, 1.5 miles southwest of Cresco.

Q. Every street in what town is named for an event or person in the life of the admiral for whom it was named?

A. Farragut (Adm. David G. Farragut).

Q. Railroad Superintendent Spaulding of England suggested the name Coggon for that town because he had what in his pocket?

A. A letter from his cousin, Wm. Coggon from Sheffield, England.

Q. What three rivers create the state's eastern and western boundaries?

A. Big Sioux, Missouri, and Mississippi.

Q. What county has the highest elevation in the state at 1,670 feet?

A. Osceola.

Q. What is the state's oldest city?

A. Dubuque.

Q. Where was Elk Horn's Danish Windmill built?

A. Norre Snede, Denmark.

Q. How large are Iowa townships?

A. Six miles square.

Q. A replica of the *Little Mermaid* statue in Copenhagen Harbor can be seen in what town?

A. Kimballton.

Q. What county had the oldest county courthouse in use in the state (second oldest in the nation)?

A. Van Buren.

Q. The Iowa State Patrol has how many district offices?

A. 15.

Q. What town was named after a heavy piece of machinery that fell in a creek and was lost?

A. Cylinder.

Q. The two farms given to Abraham Lincoln for his services in the Black Hawk War of 1832 were near what two present-day towns?

A. Garwin and Denison.

Q. Where was the first public high school in Iowa?

A. Tipton.

Q. What town was named because an early resident, Mrs. James Baker, had a fondness for a Scottish song?

A. Afton ("Flow Gently, Sweet Afton").

Q. In what town is Winnebago Industries located?

A. Forest City.

Q. Where is Iowa's only log-constructed welcome center?

A. Harrison County.

Q. What was the only fort ever built by the U.S. government to protect one Indian tribe from another?

A. Fort Atkinson.

Q. The Iowa District was first placed under the laws of the United States in 1834 by being annexed to what territory?

A. Territory of Michigan.

Q. Crown Prince Haakon of Norway visited what city on June 10, 1999 as part of its sesquicentennial celebration?

A. Decorah.

Q. What town bills itself as 857 Friendly People and One Old Grump?

A. Readlyn.

Q. What was the original name of Madrid in Boone county?

A. Swede Point.

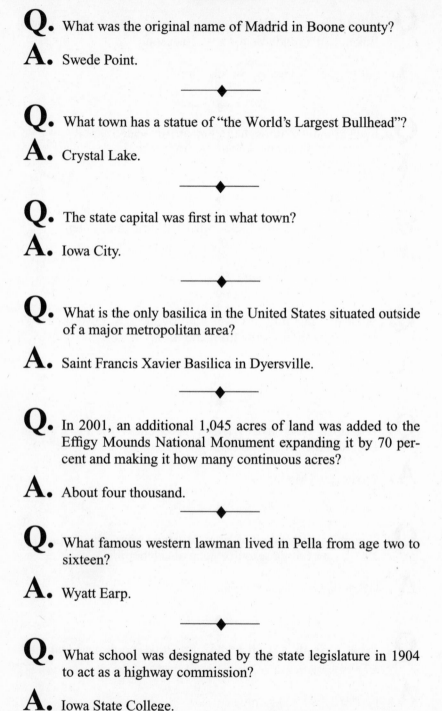

Q. What town has a statue of "the World's Largest Bullhead"?

A. Crystal Lake.

Q. The state capital was first in what town?

A. Iowa City.

Q. What is the only basilica in the United States situated outside of a major metropolitan area?

A. Saint Francis Xavier Basilica in Dyersville.

Q. In 2001, an additional 1,045 acres of land was added to the Effigy Mounds National Monument expanding it by 70 percent and making it how many continuous acres?

A. About four thousand.

Q. What famous western lawman lived in Pella from age two to sixteen?

A. Wyatt Earp.

Q. What school was designated by the state legislature in 1904 to act as a highway commission?

A. Iowa State College.

Q. What town in northeast Iowa has the largest ethnic museum in the United States?

A. Decorah.

------◆------

Q. The Mormon settlement Rushville became the town of Coonville but is now known by what name?

A. Glenwood.

------◆------

Q. What is the largest body of water in the state?

A. Rathbun Dam and Reservoir.

------◆------

Q. What was the former name of Monroe County?

A. Kishkekosh.

------◆------

Q. What part of the state is known as "the Nursery Capital of the World"?

A. Southwest Iowa.

------◆------

Q. Iowa became part of the United States after what famous land deal with France?

A. Louisiana Purchase.

------◆------

Q. Of the original twelve national cemeteries designated by Congress at the same time as Arlington, which one is in Iowa?

A. Keokuk National Cemetery.

Q. The "world's smallest church," Saint Anthony of Padua Chapel (12 ft. x 16 ft.), is in what town?

A. Festina.

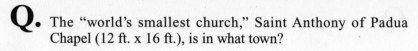

Q. How many miles wide is Iowa from east to west?

A. 324.

Q. What town in Wright County has Bain-de-la Roche, France, as its sister city?

A. Woolstock.

Q. What Mitchell County town is known as "the City of the Beautiful Maples"?

A. Osage.

Q. What county was named in honor of the only U.S. vice president elected by the Senate?

A. Johnson (Richard Mentor Johnson).

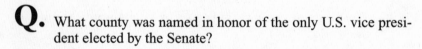

Q. What town was called Belpre (from *belle* and *prairie*) when it became the county seat in 1856?

A. Grundy Center.

Q. What was the nickname of Algona's first school, a dugout in the side of a bluff walled with logs and covered with sod?

A. Gopher College.

Q. What is the largest glacier-created lake in the state?

A. Spirit Lake.

———◆———

Q. In what ten-year period did the population of Iowa grow by 345.8 percent?

A. 1840–1850.

———◆———

Q. What is the meaning of *Amana,* selected from Song of Solomon 4:8?

A. "To remain faithful."

———◆———

Q. Where is the German Hausbarn and historical farmstead?

A. Manning.

———◆———

Q. Where is the runway of the Laurens airport?

A. On a fairway of the Laurens Golf and Country Club.

———◆———

Q. Dubuque's town clock has been tolling since what year?

A. 1873.

———◆———

Q. Penoach was the original name of what town?

A. Adel.

Q. Iowa has more miles of roads than how many other states?

A. Forty.

Q. The citizens of what town wanted it to be named Missouri Dale when it was incorporated?

A. Modale.

Q. Where is Montauk, the only furnished home built by an Iowa governor that is open as a museum?

A. Clermont.

Q. What county was named after a Hungarian patriot?

A. Kossuth.

Q. What town is "the Home Laundry Appliance Center of the World"?

A. Newton.

Q. What was the name of Julien Dubuque's land claim?

A. The Mines of Spain.

Q. What was the Indian name for Keokuk, meaning "where the water runs shallow"?

A. Puck-e-she-tuck.

Q. What four towns make up the Quad Cities?

A. Bettendorf and Davenport, Iowa, and Moline and Rock Island, Illinois.

Q. What is the state nickname?

A. The Hawkeye State.

Q. In what city is the Bayliss Park Fountain, one of the Midwest's finest lighted, computerized fountains?

A. Council Bluffs.

Q. In the late 1890s, two bank presidents from what town each tried to outdo the other by building a hotel on "his" side of town?

A. Forest City.

Q. The state legislature changed the name of what town by spelling it with a *C* instead of an *S*?

A. Centerville.

Q. What town is in three counties and at the intersection of four townships?

A. Sheldahl.

Q. Where can you find the sculpture *The Promise of America*, which honors Norwegian-American immigrants?

A. Lake Mills.

Q. For years the chamber of commerce of what town used the slogan "Next to the largest city in Iowa!"?

A. West Des Moines.

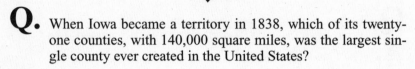

Q. When Iowa became a territory in 1838, which of its twenty-one counties, with 140,000 square miles, was the largest single county ever created in the United States?

A. Fayette.

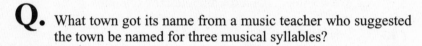

Q. What town got its name from a music teacher who suggested the town be named for three musical syllables?

A. Ladora.

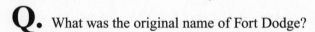

Q. What city has the only county courthouse with a gold dome?

A. Dubuque.

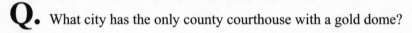

Q. What was the original name of Fort Dodge?

A. Fort Clarke.

Q. Where is Liberty Hall Historic Center, home of the family of Joseph Smith III, the first president of the Reorganized Church of Jesus Christ of Latter Day Saints?

A. Lamoni.

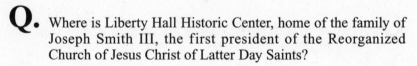

Q. Where was the first bridge to cross the Mississippi into Iowa?

A. Davenport.

Q. Besides Paris, France, what is the only other city to have its government buildings on an island in the center of the city?

A. Cedar Rapids.

———◆———

Q. What town in Tama County was originally named Iuka?

A. Tama.

———◆———

Q. What was the original name of Hamilton County?

A. Yell.

———◆———

Q. Iowa Falls in Hardin County was once called by what name?

A. Rocksylvania.

———◆———

Q. Bettendorf went by what name until 1902?

A. Gilberttown.

———◆———

Q. According to the 2000 census, what is the smallest city in the state, with a population of eleven?

A. Beaconsfield (but they claim there are 19).

———◆———

Q. Where can one see the thirty-foot-high, forty-five-ton statue of Albert the Bull?

A. Audubon.

Q. What counties don't have a single stoplight?

A. Clayton and Van Buren.

Q. How many closely united villages compose the Amana Colonies?

A. Seven—East Amana, West Amana, High Amana, Middle Amana, South Amana, Amana, and Homestead.

Q. What town name translated means "there are bears"?

A. Maquoketa.

Q. Railroad owner and avid hunter Charles Whitehead named what three towns along his railway for three of his favorite prey?

A. Mallard, Plover, and Curlew.

Q. With a depth of 136 feet, what is the deepest natural lake in the state?

A. West Okoboji.

Q. What town, named for a Winnebago chief, means "thunder" in the Winnebago tongue and "spirit" in Sioux?

A. Waukon.

Q. What town was named after John I. Blair's dog?

A. Colo.

Q. What kind of animal was Dexter named after?

A. Race horse.

———◆———

Q. What town was named after the first letters of the surnames of the eight most prominent citizens?

A. Primghar.

———◆———

Q. Zebulon Pike climbed his first Pike's Peak in Clayton County in what year?

A. 1805.

———◆———

Q. What town was named for one of its founders, Archer Dumond, and his daughter, who was the belle of the community?

A. Belmond.

———◆———

Q. In April 1994 what city was officially proclaimed "the Ice Cream Capital of the World" by the Iowa legislature?

A. Le Mars.

———◆———

Q. How many years did it take to survey what is now the state of Iowa?

A. Twenty-three.

———◆———

Q. What is the oldest bridge in Madison County?

A. Imes Bridge.

Q. What is the name of the one-hundred-foot white stone obelisk near Sioux City?

A. Floyd's Monument.

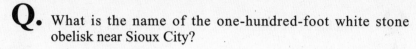

Q. The fork of the Raccoon and Des Moines Rivers is the location of what city?

A. Des Moines.

Q. What town was formerly called Bloomington?

A. Muscatine.

Q. In 1834 the Iowa District was divided into how many counties?

A. Two, DuBuque and DeMoines.

Q. Why is Stanton known as "Little White City"?

A. Every house is painted predominantly white.

Q. What does the name *Pella* mean?

A. "City of refuge."

Q. What did pioneers call the double-furrow trail that Alex McCready and his son plowed in 1856 between Fort Dodge and Sioux City?

A. The Great Road.

Q. What town's slogan is Not Down Under But Right on Top?

A. Melbourne.

———————◆———————

Q. Council Bluffs's unusual historic county jail has what nick-name?

A. The Squirrel Cage.

———————◆———————

Q. What river takes its name from the Indian word for "white potatoes"?

A. Wapsipinicon.

———————◆———————

Q. On a direct north-south line between the Lake of the Woods and the Gulf of Mexico, what is the highest point?

A. Iron Mine Hill (in Allamakee County).

———————◆———————

Q. Wahkaw County was the former name of what county?

A. Woodbury.

———————◆———————

Q. What town received its name because so many of its pioneer settlers were members of the Masonic Order?

A. Mason City.

———————◆———————

Q. What town is named for an Indian chief who aided settlers during the Black Hawk War?

A. Decorah.

Q. In 1851 where did a pioneer merchant build a store half in Missouri and half in Iowa?

A. Lineville.

Q. What was Iowa's first national monument?

A. Effigy Mounds.

Q. The town name Titonka is derived from an Indian word meaning what?

A. "Big black," the Sioux name for buffalo.

Q. How did Bloomfield get its name?

A. It was pulled out of a hat.

Q. Iowa's longest and highest bridge crosses what body of water?

A. Red Rock Lake.

Q. What city has a sister city affiliation with Eisenach, Germany, the home of Wartburg Castle?

A. Waverly.

Q. Iowans refer to what section of the state as "the Switzerland of America"?

A. The northeast.

Q. On what campus is the fifty-bell Stanton Memorial Carillon located?

A. Iowa State University.

Q. Named for the German inventor of movable type, what town was misspelled in the plat?

A. Guttenberg.

Q. Where was the first consolidated school established in 1896?

A. Buffalo Center.

Q. During World War I the name Lakota was given to what existing town?

A. Germania.

Q. In 1836 when Michigan became a state, Iowa became a part of what newly created territory?

A. Wisconsin Territory.

Q. Where is the largest Danish settlement in the United States?

A. Elk Horn.

Q. What town's population plummeted from eight thousand to one thousand after the Mormons left in 1852?

A. Kanesville (Council Bluffs since 1853).

Q. The big coal deposit in the area inspired the name of what town in Adams County?

A. Carbon.

Q. What was the first land-grant college in the nation?

A. Iowa State University.

Q. The Three Rivers Trail, which crosses Humboldt County, refers to what three rivers?

A. The West and East Forks of the Des Moines River and the Boone River.

Q. What is a simple definition of the word *loess,* as found in the Loess Hills region of western Iowa?

A. Windblown silt or dust.

Q. The town of Reinbeck derives its name from a German word with what meaning?

A. "Happy stream" or "brook."

Q. What town in Cherokee County was named for one of the sons of railroad builder John I. Blair?

A. Marcus.

Q. Between which two rivers is Grinnell situated?

A. Iowa and Skunk.

Q. What town was named for Orrin Sage of Ware, Massachusetts, a banker who helped finance its establishment?

A. Osage.

Q. Low Moor was named for what imported English product that was piled beside the railroad track?

A. Steel rails.

Q. A famous rock inspired the name of what town in Cerro Gordo County?

A. Plymouth.

Q. A young girl who confronted a murderer and saved the lives of her brothers is honored by what county name?

A. Louisa.

Q. Dublin, Ireland, is the sister city to what Iowa town?

A. Emmetsburg.

Q. Markers of what shape are used to designate historical and recreational areas along the Great River Road?

A. Pilot wheel.

Q. A historical section called Czech Village and the National Czech and Slovak Museum are in what city?

A. Cedar Rapids.

Q. Which county is bordered on three sides by water?

A. Lee (Mississippi, Des Moines, and Skunk Rivers).

◆

Q. What was the first fort in Iowa?

A. Fort Madison.

◆

Q. At sixteen miles, what is the longest natural lake in the state?

A. East Okoboji.

◆

Q. Established in 1851, Calhoun County first had what name?

A. Fox.

◆

Q. Where does Iowa rank in land mass compared to the other forty-nine states?

A. Twenty-fifth.

◆

Q. What town was named after a historian who acknowledged the honor by giving the town fifty books as the nucleus of a library?

A. Bancroft.

◆

Q. What county is known as "the Covered Bridge Capital of Iowa"?

A. Madison (with six covered bridges).

Q. Which county has two county courthouses but only one county seat?

A. Pottawattamie (in Council Bluffs, the county seat & in Avoca).

———◆———

Q. The last streetcar to operate in the state, Streetcar Number 381, ran between what two towns?

A. Waterloo and Cedar Falls.

———◆———

Q. What is the distance in miles between Iowa's northern and southern borders?

A. 210.

———◆———

Q. Risley and Yell Counties were combined to make what county?

A. Webster.

———◆———

Q. What town was named after Judge John Eckman's daughter?

A. Exira.

———◆———

Q. What was the original name of West Des Moines?

A. Valley Junction.

———◆———

Q. What town is the Black Dirt Capital of the World?

A. Conrad.

Q. What does the name *Sioux* mean?

A. "Little snakes."

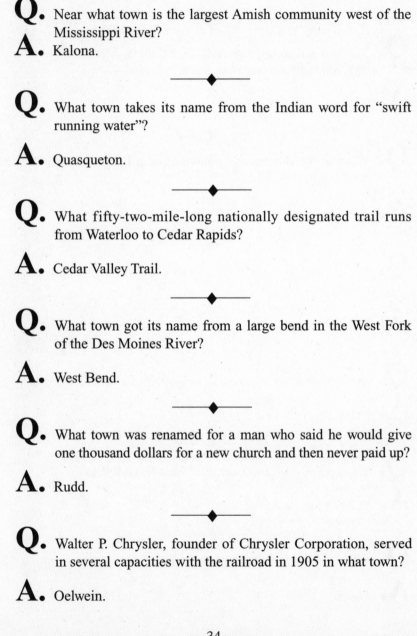

Q. Near what town is the largest Amish community west of the Mississippi River?

A. Kalona.

Q. What town takes its name from the Indian word for "swift running water"?

A. Quasqueton.

Q. What fifty-two-mile-long nationally designated trail runs from Waterloo to Cedar Rapids?

A. Cedar Valley Trail.

Q. What town got its name from a large bend in the West Fork of the Des Moines River?

A. West Bend.

Q. What town was renamed for a man who said he would give one thousand dollars for a new church and then never paid up?

A. Rudd.

Q. Walter P. Chrysler, founder of Chrysler Corporation, served in several capacities with the railroad in 1905 in what town?

A. Oelwein.

Q. Which is Iowa's youngest and smallest county?

A. Osceola (organized in 1871; 398 sq. miles).

———◆———

Q. The name of what river in southwest Iowa comes from the Indian word meaning "river crossed by boat"?

A. Nishnabotna.

———◆———

Q. What is the name of the house built by Robert Lucas, the first governor of the Iowa Territory?

A. Plum Grove.

———◆———

Q. Independence and Summerset were originally suggested as names for what town?

A. Winterset.

———◆———

Q. The state's lowest elevation point at 480 feet is in what county?

A. Lee.

———◆———

Q. What six states border Iowa?

A. Illinois, Minnesota, Wisconsin, South Dakota, Nebraska, and Missouri.

———◆———

Q. What is the tallest building in Iowa?

A. The Principal Financial Group Building (44 stories).

Q. With a population of 120,758, what is Iowa's second-largest city?

A. Cedar Rapids.

Q. What town name means "white fawn" and was the name of the daughter of a Winnebago chief?

A. Anamosa.

Q. What county seat town has the smallest population?

A. Primghar (891).

Q. Why is the interstate highway being built across eastern Iowa called "Avenue of the Saints"?

A. It will eventually link St. Paul and St. Louis.

Q. What does the Sac Indian name *Keokuk* mean?

A. "Watchful fox."

Q. What town for many years was called Sturgis Falls after the man who founded it?

A. Cedar Falls.

Q. In the late 1800s what county was the home of the Blackhawk Mineral Springs and Hospital of Magnetic and Eclectic Cure of Chronic Diseases?

A. Davis (Salt Creek Township).

Q. What town was originally called Altus because, according to railroad surveyors, it was the highest point between Des Moines and Keokuk?

A. Altoona.

Q. What is the longest bridge in Madison County?

A. Holliwell Bridge.

Q. What is the name of the twenty-one-mile trail that stretches from Crapo Park to Geode State Park?

A. Sho-Quo-Quon Trail.

Q. What county is named for the only Roman Catholic to sign the Declaration of Independence?

A. Carroll (for Charles Carroll of Carrollton, Maryland, who was also the longest living signer).

Q. For whom were the towns of Alta and Aurelia named?

A. The daughters of John I. Blair.

Q. What town name translated means "the last of the beautiful"?

A. Oskaloosa.

Q. A settlement of Mesquakie Indians can be found near what town?

A. Tama.

Q. Appanoose County was named for a Sac Indian chief whose name means what?

A. "Chief when a child."

Q. What is the meaning of *chicaqua,* the Native American term for an area of the Skunk River in Jasper County?

A. "Offensive odor."

Q. What is the third-largest city in Iowa?

A. Davenport (pop. 98,359).

Q. Which county has two county seats?

A. Lee (Fort Madison and Keokuk).

Q. What town in Clarke County was named for a Black Drink Seminole warrior?

A. Osceola.

Q. What town is known as "the Community of Flags" because of its year-round display of the flags of the fifty states?

A. Brooklyn.

ENTERTAINMENT

C H A P T E R   T W O

Q. In the movie *Field of Dreams,* what was Kevin Costner's response to the question, "Is this heaven?"

A. "No. It's Iowa."

---◆---

Q. Johnny Carson's grandfather, C. N. "Kit" Carson was mayor of what town from 1944–48?

A. Logan.

---◆---

Q. Who was born Louie Weertz and graduated from Des Moines' North High School in 1942?

A. Pianist Roger Williams.

---◆---

Q. What *NBC Nightly News* anchorman attended the University of Iowa?

A. Tom Brokaw.

---◆---

Q. What movie, based on a Johnny Paycheck hit song, was filmed in Des Moines in 1980?

A. *Take This Job and Shove It.*

Q. What famous late-night television host was born in Corning in 1925?

A. Johnny Carson.

Q. What 1953 Oscar winner for *From Here to Eternity* and star of her own television show was born in Denison in 1921?

A. Donna Reed (1921–86).

Q. What is singer Andy Williams' actual first name?

A. Howard.

Q. What Council Bluffs native starred in the title role of the film *Weekend at Bernie's?*

A. Terry Kiser.

Q. Forrest Tucker, who attended Casady Elementary and North High School in Des Moines, starred as Sergeant O'Rouke in what 1960s television western sitcom?

A. *F-Troop.*

Q. James Ellison (1920–93), who starred as Buffalo Bill in *The Plainsman,* was born in what town?

A. Guthrie Center.

Q. What famous brother duo, with the hits "Bye Bye Love" and "Cathy's Clown," got their professional start in Shenandoah on radio station KMA?

A. Don and Phil Everly.

Q. Who first performed "The Iowa Corn Song" in public in 1912?

A. The Des Moines Shriners.

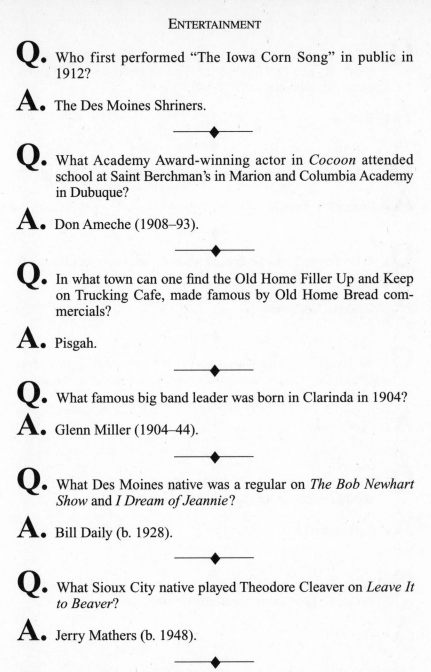

Q. What Academy Award-winning actor in *Cocoon* attended school at Saint Berchman's in Marion and Columbia Academy in Dubuque?

A. Don Ameche (1908–93).

Q. In what town can one find the Old Home Filler Up and Keep on Trucking Cafe, made famous by Old Home Bread commercials?

A. Pisgah.

Q. What famous big band leader was born in Clarinda in 1904?

A. Glenn Miller (1904–44).

Q. What Des Moines native was a regular on *The Bob Newhart Show* and *I Dream of Jeannie*?

A. Bill Daily (b. 1928).

Q. What Sioux City native played Theodore Cleaver on *Leave It to Beaver*?

A. Jerry Mathers (b. 1948).

Q. What Burlington native played Bub on *My Three Sons* and Fred Mertz on *I Love Lucy*?

A. William Frawley (1887–1966).

Q. What director of photography, who grew up in Mount Pleasant, won two Emmys for *Raid on Entebbe* (1977) and *A Streetcar Named Desire* (1984)?

A. Wilmer "Bill" Butler, A.S.C.

Q. Who wrote the song "The Little Brown Church in the Vale"?

A. William S. Pitts.

Q. What product was advertised in 1960s television commercials by a man who said, "Nothing is better for thee, than me"?

A. Quaker Oats cereal.

Q. To honor Virginia Christine (1920–96), television's Mrs. Olson, the Stanton water tower was constructed in the shape of what kitchen appliance?

A. Coffee pot.

Q. To complement its coffee pot water tower, Stanton dedicated another water tower shaped like what?

A. Coffee cup (June 22, 2001).

Q. Winterset-born film star John Wayne won an Academy Award in 1969 for his performance in what movie?

A. *True Grit.*

Q. On what television series did Sada Thompson, born in Des Moines in 1929, play Kate Lawrence?

A. *Family.*

Q. What was the state's first television station?

A. WOC in Davenport, in 1949.

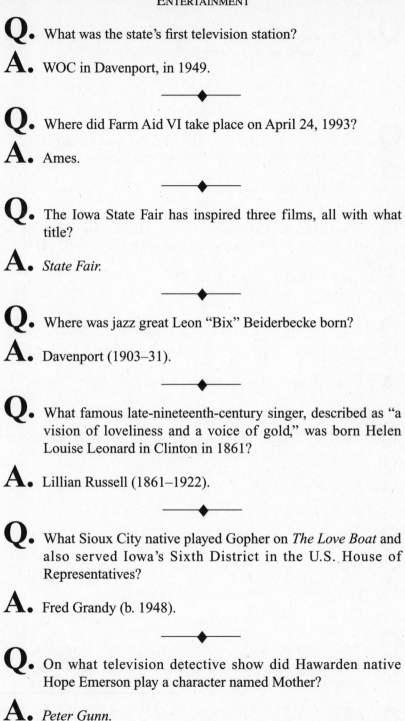

Q. Where did Farm Aid VI take place on April 24, 1993?

A. Ames.

Q. The Iowa State Fair has inspired three films, all with what title?

A. *State Fair.*

Q. Where was jazz great Leon "Bix" Beiderbecke born?

A. Davenport (1903–31).

Q. What famous late-nineteenth-century singer, described as "a vision of loveliness and a voice of gold," was born Helen Louise Leonard in Clinton in 1861?

A. Lillian Russell (1861–1922).

Q. What Sioux City native played Gopher on *The Love Boat* and also served Iowa's Sixth District in the U.S. House of Representatives?

A. Fred Grandy (b. 1948).

Q. On what television detective show did Hawarden native Hope Emerson play a character named Mother?

A. *Peter Gunn.*

Q. What title did Peggy Lee suggest that Burlington composer Bart Howard use for his song "In Other Words"?

A. "Fly Me to the Moon."

Q. What Miss Universe winner (1956) was from Ottumwa?

A. Carol Morris.

Q. What inventor is known for the first theatrical presentation of sound-on-film (1916) and the first talking newsreel (1924)?

A. Lee DeForest (Council Bluffs).

Q. What Des Moines–born actress made sixty movies including *In the Navy* (1941) with Dick Powell and Abbot & Costello?

A. Claire (Dorothy Anne) Dodd (1908–73).

Q. Based on a Mark Twain novel, what 1974 movie was filmed in Iowa along the Mississippi River?

A. *Huckleberry Finn.*

Q. Riverside claims to be the future birthplace (March 21, 2228) of what fictional character?

A. Capt. James T. Kirk of the USS *Enterprise.*

Q. What was the last name of sisters Lola, Priscilla, and Rosemary, who grew up in Indianola and costarred in a series of movies that began with *Four Daughters* in 1938?

A. Lane.

Q. What pianist got his professional start at Babe's Restaurant in Des Moines and attended Drake University?

A. Roger Williams (b. 1924).

Q. What ABC News correspondent grew up in northeast Iowa and worked at WMT in Cedar Rapids?

A. Richard Threlkeld.

Q. Just before the Prince of Wales became King Edward VII in 1901, what sleight-of-hand expert from Marshalltown taught him a few coin tricks?

A. T. Nelson Downs.

Q. What Barbara Stanwyck/Joel McCrea film was shot in Council Bluffs in 1938?

A. *Union Pacific.*

Q. What were the roles of Marshalltown's Ruth E. Smith and Dale Paullin in the 1939 film classic *The Wizard of Oz*?

A. Two of the 124 Munchkins.

Q. What animals did Ringling Brothers circus clown Felix Adler use in his act for thirty years?

A. Pigs.

Q. The 1992 television movie *The Woman Who Loved Elvis* starring Roseanne Barr was filmed in what town?

A. Ottumwa.

Q. Where did Daniel J. Travanti, star of the television series *Hill Street Blues,* grow up?

A. Dubuque.

Q. What Oscar-winning actor and star of *High Noon* was a student at Grinnell College?

A. Gary Cooper.

Q. What University of Iowa graduate played Barney Collier on television's *Mission: Impossible*?

A. Greg Morris.

Q. During the CB radio craze of the 1970s, what was the smash hit song of Audubon's C. W. McCall?

A. "Convoy."

Q. In 1971, American Republic Insurance Company of Des Moines hired what comedian to endorse its Americare 39 life insurance policy?

A. Jack Benny (policy named after his mythical age).

Q. What magician built a house in Fairfield?

A. David Copperfield.

Q. What Davenport native portrays Jack Deveraux on *Days of our Lives*?

A. Matthew Ashford (b. 1960).

Q. Where was Andy Williams, of "Moon River" fame, born in 1930?

A. Wall Lake.

———◆———

Q. Bands led by Lawrence Welk, Count Basie, and Guy Lombardo played in the dance hall of what county park in the 1930s and 40s?

A. Spring Lake Park (Greene County).

———◆———

Q. Born in LaPorte City, what children's television star played the straight woman to puppets Kukla and Oliver J. Dragon?

A. Fran Allison (1907–89).

———◆———

Q. What Woolstock native played one of the Tarleton twins in *Gone With the Wind* and was television's first Superman?

A. George Reeves (1914–59).

———◆———

Q. What Davenport native starred in the television series *MacGruder & Loud*?

A. John Getz.

———◆———

Q. What song from the musical *The Music Man* has the word *Iowa* in the title?

A. "Iowa Stubborn."

———◆———

Q. Where was the boyhood home of puppeteer Bil Baird?

A. Mason City.

Q. All the residents of what town appeared on *The Late Show* with David Letterman in 1989?

A. Bolan.

◆

Q. What television star of *Mrs. Columbo* and *Star Trek Voyager* was born in Dubuque in 1955?

A. Kate Mulgrew.

◆

Q. What Decorah native played Sharon Gless's mother in the television show *The Trials of Rosie O'Neill* and Jane Seymour's mother in the television show *Dr. Quinn, Medicine Woman*?

A. Georgann Johnson.

◆

Q. In what 1954 horror flick did Waterloo's Julie Adams play the heroine?

A. *Creature from the Black Lagoon.*

◆

Q. What movie actress (*Calvacade,* 1933 and *House of Seven Gables,* 1940) of Dubuque launched her acting career by making people think she was British?

A. Margaret Lindsay (1910–81).

◆

Q. Appearing in the 1905 production of the musical comedy *The Girl at the Helm* at the LaSalle Theater in Chicago, what were the first typewriters to appear onstage?

A. Oliver typewriters (invented and produced in Iowa).

◆

Q. Airplane N3794N that crashed, killing Buddy Holly and others, was made popular by what Don McLean song?

A. "American Pie."

Q. What Leon native played Harry O'Neill on *One Life to Live* in 1984?

A. Arlen Dean Snyder.

------◆------

Q. What Cornell College alumnus composed more than seven hundred popular songs, including "In the Shade of the Old Apple Tree"?

A. Egbert Van Alstyne.

------◆------

Q. What 1950 film was loosely based on the life of jazz cornet great Bix Beiderbecke (1903–31)?

A. *Young Man with a Horn.*

------◆------

Q. On what date, known as "the day the music died," did Buddy Holly die in a plane crash after he performed in Iowa?

A. February 3, 1959.

------◆------

Q. During the 1930s and 1940s, what Davenport native appeared in nearly one hundred films, such as *The Sign of the Cross, Northwest Passage,* and *Young Dr. Kildare*?

A. Nat Pendleton (1895–1967).

------◆------

Q. In what town did Nick Nolte, star of *Down and Out in Beverly Hills, Lorenzo's Oil,* and the miniseries *Rich Man, Poor Man,* attend elementary school?

A. Ames.

------◆------

Q. Born in Humboldt in 1959, what actor has such movie credits as *Mighty Joe Young* (1998) and *Apollo 13* (1995)?

A. Christian Clemenson.

Q. What 1938 film was shot in Anamosa?

A. *Penitentiary.*

———◆———

Q. What Davenport native starred in the films *Lolita, The Flim Flam Man,* and *The Night of the Iguana*?

A. Sue Lyon (b. 1946).

———◆———

Q. Where did the Ringling brothers grow up?

A. McGregor.

———◆———

Q. Shot in Council Bluffs and directed by Sean Penn, what 1991 film was inspired by Bruce Springsteen's song "Highway Patrol"?

A. *The Indian Runner.*

———◆———

Q. What self-proclaimed "Most Famous Hostess in the World" said she was born in the Keokuk town hall in 1883?

A. Elsa Maxwell (1883–1963).

———◆———

Q. What Audubon native sang with Kenny Rogers on the hit song "Ruby, Don't Take Your Love to Town" and later married Roger Miller?

A. Mary Arnold Miller.

———◆———

Q. The 1980 film *Pennies from Heaven* starring Steve Martin and Bernadette Peters was shot in what Iowa city?

A. Dubuque.

Q. Since what year has there been a municipal band in Oskaloosa?

A. 1864.

Q. What role did Grinnell College graduate Walter Koenig play in *Star Trek*?

A. Ens. Pavel Chekov.

Q. Sportscaster Greg Gumbel is an alumnus of what college?

A. Loras.

Q. Born Dale Bales in 1886, Bill Bailey of *Won't You Come Home, Bill Bailey* fame was born in what city?

A. Maxwell.

Q. Who made a large contribution to the Logan Community Building as a memorial to his grandfather, who was a lifelong resident?

A. Johnny Carson.

Q. Ben Pippert, the inspiration for the book and TV movie *Orphan Train,* was one of five siblings placed in homes in what community?

A. Dysart.

Q. What Des Moines native played trombone with Henry Mancini for many years?

A. Johnny Haliburten.

Q. What actress lived in Randalia and was a model in Des Moines before moving to Hollywood and becoming a regular on *CHiPs*?

A. Randi Oakes (b. 1951).

———◆———

Q. Wade on *All My Children* was played by what Fort Dodge native?

A. Marlian Fisher.

———◆———

Q. Famous for his tipsy portrayals, what comedian was a deejay at radio station KBIZ in Ottumwa?

A. Foster Brooks.

———◆———

Q. What producer of such films as *The Amityville Horror, Love at First Bite,* and *Dr. Phibes* was born in Fort Dodge in 1918?

A. Samuel Arkoff.

———◆———

Q. Meredith Willson began his professional career playing what instrument with the John Philip Sousa Band?

A. Flute.

———◆———

Q. What courthouse and its square were the setting for the 1969 Dick Van Dyke film *Cold Turkey*?

A. Winterset.

———◆———

Q. What film star of *Saint Joan* and *Paint Your Wagon* was born in Marshalltown?

A. Jean Seberg (1938–79).

Q. What Des Moines native starred in television's *Tales of the Gold Monkey*?

A. Stephen Collins (b. 1947).

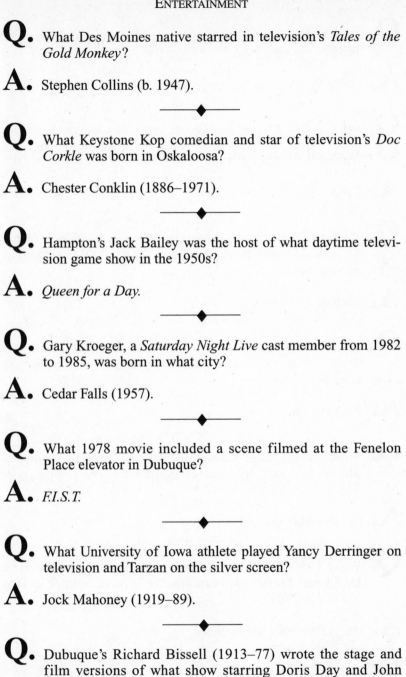

Q. What Keystone Kop comedian and star of television's *Doc Corkle* was born in Oskaloosa?

A. Chester Conklin (1886–1971).

Q. Hampton's Jack Bailey was the host of what daytime television game show in the 1950s?

A. *Queen for a Day.*

Q. Gary Kroeger, a *Saturday Night Live* cast member from 1982 to 1985, was born in what city?

A. Cedar Falls (1957).

Q. What 1978 movie included a scene filmed at the Fenelon Place elevator in Dubuque?

A. *F.I.S.T.*

Q. What University of Iowa athlete played Yancy Derringer on television and Tarzan on the silver screen?

A. Jock Mahoney (1919–89).

Q. Dubuque's Richard Bissell (1913–77) wrote the stage and film versions of what show starring Doris Day and John Raitt?

A. *Pajama Game.*

Q. What *CBS This Morning* host attended Central College in Pella?

A. Harry Smith.

———◆———

Q. What star of *Blazing Saddles, Young Frankenstein,* and *Willy Wonka and the Chocolate Factory* graduated from the University of Iowa in 1955?

A. Gene Wilder.

———◆———

Q. Brothers Gary R. And Dave Alan Johnson, producers of the TV series *Second Noah* (1996) and *DOC* (2001), are natives of what town?

A. Buffalo Center.

———◆———

Q. What star of *E.T.: The Extra-Terrestrial, Cross Creek,* and *Jagged Edge* earned a bachelor's degree in English at Grinnell College?

A. Peter Coyote.

———◆———

Q. What was the stage name of the actress, born in Clarinda as Marvel Maxwell, who starred in the films *The Lemon Drop Kid* and *Rock-a-bye Baby*?

A. Marilyn Maxwell (1921–72).

———◆———

Q. What 1950s television sitcom mom of two boys named David and Ricky was born Harriet Hilliard Snyder in Des Moines in 1909?

A. Harriet Nelson (1909–1994).

———◆———

Q. Who wrote "The Iowa Corn Song"?

A. John T. Beeston and George Hamilton.

Q. What Disney child star, who appeared in *Song of the South, So Dear to My Heart,* and *Treasure Island,* was born in Cedar Rapids?

A. Bobby Driscoll (1937–68).

Q. What politician stirred up a national controversy when he attacked network news commentaries during a televised speech from Des Moines on November 13, 1969?

A. Vice President Spiro Agnew.

Q. What Norwalk native appeared in the films *Cleopatra, The Shoes of the Fisherman, Once upon a Time in the West,* and *The Ten Commandments*?

A. John Frederick (b. 1916).

Q. The 1968 film *Gaily Gaily,* with Beau Bridges, Melina Mercouri, Brian Keith, and Margot Kidder, was filmed in what city?

A. Dubuque.

Q. What Hollywood cinematographer, who was director of photography on *Jaws, Grease,* and *One Flew Over the Cuckoo's Nest,* attended Iowa Wesleyan?

A. Wilmer Butler (b. 1931).

Q. Under the name of John Rox, what Winterset native wrote the song "It's a Big Wide Wonderful World"?

A. John Herring.

Q. John Wayne's father followed what occupation in Winterset?

A. Pharmacist.

Q. Author, comedian, and actor Steve Allen attended what university?

A. Drake.

◆

Q. What former NBC consumer reporter formerly worked at radio station KRNT in Des Moines?

A. David Horowitz.

◆

Q. What party hostess and songwriter from Keokuk invented the scavenger hunt and the treasure hunt?

A. Elsa Maxwell (1883–1963).

◆

Q. What 1983 film starring Jessica Lange and Sam Shepard was shot in Waterloo?

A. *Country.*

◆

Q. Television actor Tony Danza received a scholarship to what school?

A. University of Dubuque.

◆

Q. What actor, who played Benjamin Horne on *Twin Peaks,* was born in Avoca and starred in the films *The Diary of Anne Frank* and *West Side Story*?

A. Richard Beymer (b. 1938).

◆

Q. What Monroe County native became a cartoonist for Disney and worked on *Peter Pan, Cinderella, The Lady and the Tramp,* and *Alice in Wonderland*?

A. Dan Karpan.

Q. What Red Oak actor, who was raised in Des Moines, was known mainly for the wit and humor he put into many westerns, including *The Three Mesquiteers* and *Rough Riders* series and *Requiem for a Gunfighter*?

A. Raymond Hatton (1887–1971).

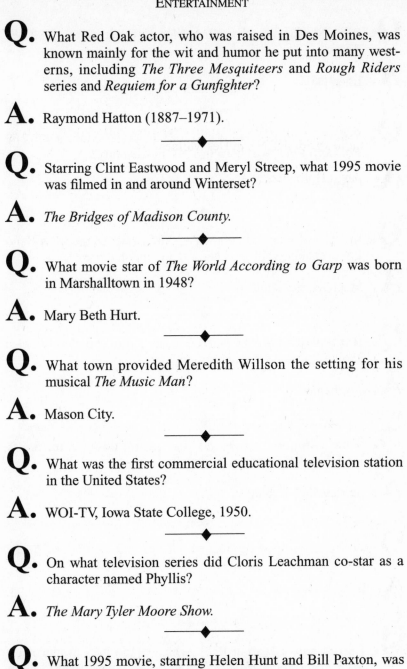

Q. Starring Clint Eastwood and Meryl Streep, what 1995 movie was filmed in and around Winterset?

A. *The Bridges of Madison County.*

Q. What movie star of *The World According to Garp* was born in Marshalltown in 1948?

A. Mary Beth Hurt.

Q. What town provided Meredith Willson the setting for his musical *The Music Man*?

A. Mason City.

Q. What was the first commercial educational television station in the United States?

A. WOI-TV, Iowa State College, 1950.

Q. On what television series did Cloris Leachman co-star as a character named Phyllis?

A. *The Mary Tyler Moore Show.*

Q. What 1995 movie, starring Helen Hunt and Bill Paxton, was filmed in central Iowa (Ames, Eldora)?

A. *Twister.*

Q. What Monticello native plays Margo Hughes on *As the World Turns*?

A. Ellen Dolan.

———◆———

Q. Stuart Margolin, who starred as Angel Martin on *The Rockford Files,* was born in 1940 in what city?

A. Davenport.

———◆———

Q. In 1921 who became known as "the Father of the Iowa Band Law," enabling cities to support a municipal band?

A. Maj. George Landers.

———◆———

Q. Bill Bailey, who once worked at the Kirkwood Hotel in Des Moines, played what instrument?

A. The banjo.

———◆———

Q. What Ottumwa native was the casting director for *South Pacific* and *Fiddler on the Roof*?

A. Shirley Rich Krohm.

———◆———

Q. David L. Wolper, producer of *Roots* and *The Thorn Birds,* attended what university?

A. Drake.

———◆———

Q. Carroll native Marian Rees, who worked as a producer on *Miss Rose White, Home Fires Burning, Foxfire,* and *Orphan Train,* graduated from what Des Moines High School?

A. Roosevelt High School.

Q. What Clinton native was the head clown for the Ringling Brothers circus and from 1919 to 1946 never missed a performance?

A. Felix Adler (1895–1960).

Q. What 1989–97 ABC television series starring Craig T. Nelson filmed scenes several times in Iowa City?

A. *Coach.*

Q. In 1964 what jazz singer and 1982 Grammy winner received a master's degree from the University of Iowa?

A. Al Jarreau.

Q. What type of business did Jean Seberg's parents operate in Marshalltown?

A. A drugstore.

Q. The lives of five brothers from Waterloo who joined the navy were the subject of what 1944 film?

A. *The Fighting Sullivans.*

Q. What star of the 1960s television series *Hazel* was born in Cedar Rapids in 1913?

A. Don Defore (1913–93).

Q. Born in Cedar Rapids in 1963, what was Terry Farrell's role in the TV series *Deep Space Nine* (1992–99)?

A. Lt. Comdr. Jadzia Dax.

Q. Born in Council Bluffs in 1884, what film comedian was considered one of the big four of the silent film era along with Charlie Chaplin, Buster Keaton, and Harold Lloyd?

A. Harry Langdon (1884–1944).

◆

Q. The 1933 film version of *State Fair* starred what famous American humorist?

A. Will Rogers.

◆

Q. In what year did the state's first commercial radio station, WOC, begin operation in Davenport?

A. 1922.

◆

Q. What late-night talk show host aired a show in 1980 from the home of Cresco's Jane Goldworthy?

A. David Letterman.

◆

Q. Where was Sharon Farrell, who plays Flo Webster on *The Young and Restless,* born?

A. Sioux City (b. 1946).

◆

Q. On what television series did Des Moines native David Anthony Higgins (b. 1961) portray Joe Farrell?

A. *Ellen.*

◆

Q. What Creston native played receptionist Carol Kester on *The Bob Newhart Show*?

A. Marcia Wallace (b. 1942).

Q. Born Edward Vance Flanagan in Fort Madison in 1908, what movie star appeared in *Topper Returns* and *Brewster's Millions*?

A. Dennis O'Keefe (1908–68).

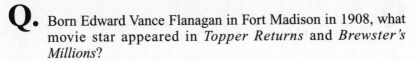

Q. In *It's a Wonderful Life,* what was the first name of the character portrayed by Iowa's Donna Reed?

A. Mary.

Q. What comedian, writer, and actor born in Ottumwa was once married to Roseanne Barr?

A. Tom Arnold (b. 1959).

Q. What graduate of Central College has anchored ABC's *Good Morning, America* and hosted *Timeline*?

A. Steve Bell.

Q. Annabeth Gish, star of *Mystic Pizza, Wyatt Earp,* and *Desert Bloom,* attended what high school in Cedar Falls?

A. Northern University High School.

Q. What Pleasantville native appeared in the films *Duel in the Sun, Kiss and Tell,* and *A Guest in the House*?

A. Scott McKay (1922–87).

Q. What 1967 film starring Harry Dean Stanton and John Carradine was shot entirely in the state?

A. *The Hostage.*

Q. What famous pianist donated a grand piano to the Danish Immigrant Museum in Elk Horn?

A. Victor Borge.

◆

Q. In what Dubuque theater did Al Jolson and Eddie Cantor perform during the days of vaudeville?

A. The Five Flags Theater (formerly the Orpheum).

◆

Q. What was the occupation of Johnny Carson's father when Johnny was born in Iowa?

A. Area manager of the Iowa-Nebraska Power and Light Company.

◆

Q. Known as "the King of Jazz," what band conductor often spent his summers in Bedford with his grandparents?

A. Paul Whiteman.

◆

Q. What Strawberry Point native was in the films *Back to the Future* and *Top Gun*?

A. David Tolkon.

◆

Q. What Sioux City native was in the films *Calamity Jane* and *Mister Roberts,* played Philip Marlowe on television, and starred as Tom Horton on *Days of Our Lives*?

A. Macdonald Carey (1913–94).

◆

Q. How many Ringling brothers were there?

A. Seven. Albert, Otto, Alfred, Charles, and John started out with penny circuses in McGregor. The other two brothers were Henry and August.

Q. What Lourdes native was an accomplished clarinetist whose nicknames included "Jerkwater Jazzmaker" and "King of Korn"?

A. Freddie Fisher (1904–67).

Q. At what age did Donna Reed leave her hometown of Denison by train to go to Hollywood?

A. Sixteen.

Q. What Cedar Rapids native played Jean Smart's television husband on *Designing Women*?

A. Douglas Barr (b. 1949).

Q. Ron Clements, director of *Hercules* (1977), *Aladdin* (1992), and *The Little Mermaid* (1989), was born in what town?

A. Sioux City (1953).

Q. What is the name of the little boy who "likes it" in the commercials for Life cereal (produced by Iowa's Quaker Oats Co.)?

A. Mikey.

Q. What 1991 film starring Carol Burnett and Michael Caine was shot in Des Moines?

A. *Noises Off.*

Q. What were the first names of the five Cherry Sisters, a vaudeville act so bad they became popular?

A. Ellie, Lizzie, Effie, Addie, and Jessie.

Q. What Iowa City native was in the movies *National Lampoon's Class Reunion* and *The Incredible Shrinking Woman*?

A. Randolph Powell (b. 1950).

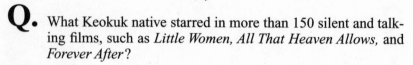

Q. What Keokuk native starred in more than 150 silent and talking films, such as *Little Women, All That Heaven Allows,* and *Forever After*?

A. Conrad Nagel (1897–1970).

Q. What was John Wayne's birth name?

A. Marion Robert Morrison (1907–1979).

Q. Actor Cary Grant died of a stroke November 29, 1986 in what town?

A. Davenport.

Q. Alf Ringling was a juggler and acrobat, but what farm implement could he balance on his chin?

A. Plow.

Q. What 1989 baseball movie starring Kevin Costner was filmed in an Iowa cornfield?

A. *Field of Dreams.*

Q. Soaps actor Mark Pinter, who plays Roger Smythe on *All My Children,* was born in what town?

A. Decorah (1950).

Q. The 1987 film *Miles from Home,* starring Richard Gere, Penelope Ann Miller, Laurie Metcalf, and Helen Hunt, was filmed in what city?

A. Cedar Rapids.

Q. What Clear Lake native was in the films *Grease, Grease 2,* and *Don't Stop the Music?*

A. Dick Patterson (1929–99).

Q. What guitarist/songwriter for the original Alice Cooper group is interred at Evergreen Cemetery in Clarion?

A. Glen Buxton, The Blond Bomber (1947–77).

Q. During the early 1900s, what famous Chautauqua quartet used "The Church in the Wildwood" as their theme song?

A. The Weatherwax Brothers.

Q. A Stephen King horror story served as the basis for what 1983 film shot in Whiting?

A. *Children of the Corn.*

Q. What Griswold actor played Reese Bennett on *Laredo* (1965–67) and was in *Tora! Tora! Tora!* (1970)?

A. Neville Brand (1920–92).

Q. What Davenport native plays Sally Gleason on *The Guiding Light?*

A. Patricia Barry (b. 1930).

Q. Depicted in the 1999 movie *The Straight Story,* Alvin Straight traveled, in 1994, from Laurens, Iowa to Mt. Zion, Wisconsin riding what?

A. His 1966 lawn mower.

◆

Q. Who starred as Iowa's Glenn Miller in *The Glenn Miller Story*?

A. James Stewart.

◆

Q. What television series starred former University of Iowa football star Alex Karras as the godfather of Emmanuel Lewis?

A. *Webster.*

◆

Q. Cloris Leachman, who was born in Des Moines in 1926, won an Oscar for what film?

A. *The Last Picture Show.*

◆

Q. What *Melrose Place* star was born in Iowa City?

A. Laura Leighton (b. 1968).

◆

Q. At what Des Moines restaurant did Marilyn Maye, a regular performer on *The Tonight Show* with Johnny Carson, begin her career?

A. Babe's Restaurant.

◆

Q. In what town did Buddy Holly, Ritchie Valens, and J. P. "the Big Bopper" Richardson perform their last concert?

A. Clear Lake at The Surf Ballroom.

HISTORY

C H A P T E R   T H R E E

Q. Who invented the first visible typewriter in Dyersville in 1894 and reproduced it at his typewriter factory in Epworth?

A. Rev. Thomas Oliver.

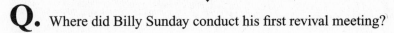

Q. Where did Billy Sunday conduct his first revival meeting?

A. Garner.

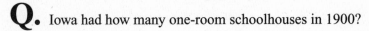

Q. Iowa had how many one-room schoolhouses in 1900?

A. 12,623.

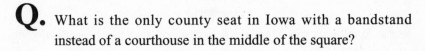

Q. What is the only county seat in Iowa with a bandstand instead of a courthouse in the middle of the square?

A. Oskaloosa.

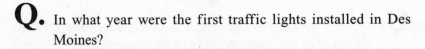

Q. In what year were the first traffic lights installed in Des Moines?

A. 1926.

Q. What self-contained French settlement had the theme "One for all and all for one," and was the longest existing secular, purely communal group in American history?

A. Icaria.

Q. The last battle in Iowa between Native American tribes took place in 1854 between the Sioux and Winnebago near what town?

A. Rolfe.

Q. In 1877 William H. Voss built the first hand-operated washing machine in what city?

A. Davenport.

Q. How did Carlisle's Bobbi McCaughey make history on November 19, 1997?

A. Birthed first surviving septuplets (3 girls, 4 boys).

Q. The first wedding in Iowa, that of William Ross and Matilda Morg, took place in what town?

A. Burlington.

Q. Who built the Algona Nativity scene that has been displayed since 1945?

A. World War II German prisoners of war.

Q. In 1905 the Jefferson city council passed an ordinance establishing what maximum speed limit for automobiles in the city?

A. Eight miles per hour.

Q. James "Tama Jim" Wilson, secretary of agriculture under three presidents, emigrated from Scotland in 1855 to a farm near what town?

A. Traer.

Q. Who has been nationally honored as "the Mother of 4-H"?

A. Jessie Field.

Q. What town has a cemetery with a monument for each war, beginning with the Civil War and concluding with Desert Storm?

A. Carroll.

Q. Iowa ranks where among the fifty states for percentage of its population having undergraduate degrees?

A. First.

Q. In what year was the first railroad bridge built across the Mississippi River?

A. 1856.

Q. Grinnell College began as Iowa College in what town?

A. Davenport.

Q. In what year was corporal punishment in schools banned by the legislature?

A. 1989.

Q. Because three honey trees were chopped down in a border dispute between Iowa and Missouri, an 1839 incident was known by what name?

A. The Honey War.

———◆———

Q. What two Iowa women became first ladies of the nation?

A. Lou Henry Hoover and Mamie Doud Eisenhower.

———◆———

Q. David H. Clark, the first white child born in Iowa, was born April 21, 1834, in what town?

A. Buffalo (between Burlington & Dubuque).

———◆———

Q. In what year did the first McDonald's restaurant open in Iowa?

A. 1958 (in Davenport).

———◆———

Q. What was the state theme that Gov. Robert Ray adopted in 1970?

A. "Iowa, a place to grow."

———◆———

Q. In what year did the Iowa State College of Agriculture and Mechanic Arts become Iowa State University of Science and Technology?

A. 1959.

———◆———

Q. Established in 1867, what was the first life insurance company in Iowa?

A. Equitable Life of Iowa.

Q. Arthur J. Hartman made the first recorded airplane flight in Iowa on the Burlington golf course in what year?

A. 1910 (it rose ten feet).

———◆———

Q. Who founded a packing company in Ottumwa in 1878?

A. John H. Morrell.

———◆———

Q. Billing himself as "the Human Fly," who tried to climb the Davis County courthouse in 1924, fell, and then climbed it successfully in 1932?

A. Henry Poland.

———◆———

Q. In the early days of auto travel, what name was given to Highway 6 between Des Moines and Council Bluffs?

A. The Great White Way.

———◆———

Q. During World War II, where was the first and principal training center for the Women's Army Corps (WAC) located?

A. Fort Des Moines.

———◆———

Q. Who was the first governor of the state?

A. Ansel Briggs.

———◆———

Q. To what Indian nation did the Iowa tribe belong?

A. Sioux.

Q. What secret club was begun by six female students at Iowa Wesleyan College in 1869?

A. PEO (a philanthropic educational organization that keeps the actual meaning of the letters secret within the organization.)

◆

Q. In what year did Fort Madison publisher James G. Edward promote the nickname "Hawkeyes" for Iowans?

A. 1838.

◆

Q. Whose gang robbed passengers of the Rock Island train west of Adair in 1873?

A. Jesse James.

◆

Q. What town did the Amana Society purchase because it had a railroad?

A. Homestead.

◆

Q. West Branch-born Herbert Hoover was elected president in what year?

A. 1928.

◆

Q. In what year was the first telephone line built in Iowa?

A. 1877.

◆

Q. What Sioux Citian lived in the White House from 1940–42?

A. Harry Hopkins.

Q. What is the state motto?

A. "Our liberties we prize and our rights we will maintain."

◆

Q. What Iowan was secretary of the interior in 1865 under President Andrew Johnson?

A. James Harlan.

◆

Q. Who was the state's first millionaire?

A. Benjamin Franklin Allen.

◆

Q. What company manufactures cotton pickers and grain drills in Ankeny?

A. John Deere.

◆

Q. Who was elected president of the Mormon Church in Kanesville in 1847?

A. Brigham Young.

◆

Q. On what historic day were trees, which are still alive, planted at Main and First St. South in Maynard?

A. The day President Lincoln was assassinated (April 14, 1865).

◆

Q. What is the name of the oldest building on the Iowa State University campus?

A. The Farm House Museum.

Q. What famous foreign leader visited the farm of Roswell Garst in 1959?

A. Nikita S. Khruschev.

Q. At age sixty-six, who was Iowa's oldest governor at the time of his inauguration?

A. Francis M. Drake.

Q. What graduate of Iowa Wesleyan became the first female attorney in the United States in 1869?

A. Arabella Babb Mansfield.

Q. What is the name of the nation's biggest warship, the fifth most decorated of the sixty-one battleships in American history?

A. The USS *Iowa*.

Q. In what war did more Iowa troops, per capita, see action than soldiers from any other state?

A. Civil War (76,000).

Q. On what date did Iowa become a state?

A. December 28, 1846.

Q. How old was Kate Shelley when she crawled across a bridge near Moingona during a storm in 1881 to warn a passenger train of a collapsed bridge?

A. Fifteen.

Q. What company manufactured the nation's first tractors?

A. The Hart-Parr Company.

Q. How many types of marble are in the interior of the state capitol?

A. Twenty-nine.

Q. What Iowan was vice president, secretary of agriculture, and secretary of commerce under President Franklin Roosevelt?

A. Henry A. Wallace.

Q. Who was the first Iowan killed in World War I?

A. Merle Hay.

Q. Who was involved in the Iowa Supreme Court case that established "fair comment and criticism" as an important principle of libel law?

A. The Cherry Sisters of Marion.

Q. Iowa led the nation in reviving the nineteenth century tradition of riverboat gambling in what year?

A. 1991.

Q. What national labor leader was born in 1880 in the coal-mining camp of Cleveland, a mile east of Lucas?

A. John L. Lewis.

Q. In 1958 how many one-room, public, rural elementary schools were there?

A. Five thousand.

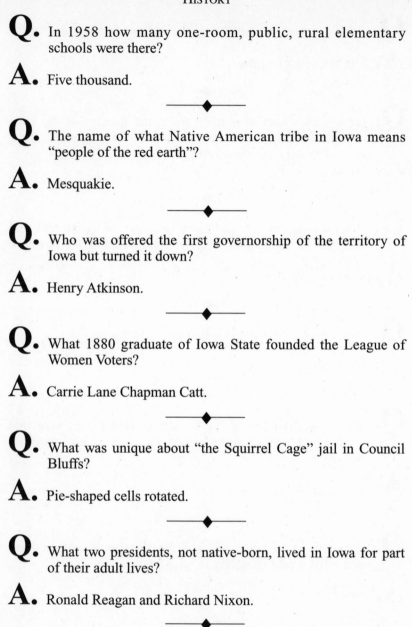

Q. The name of what Native American tribe in Iowa means "people of the red earth"?

A. Mesquakie.

Q. Who was offered the first governorship of the territory of Iowa but turned it down?

A. Henry Atkinson.

Q. What 1880 graduate of Iowa State founded the League of Women Voters?

A. Carrie Lane Chapman Catt.

Q. What was unique about "the Squirrel Cage" jail in Council Bluffs?

A. Pie-shaped cells rotated.

Q. What two presidents, not native-born, lived in Iowa for part of their adult lives?

A. Ronald Reagan and Richard Nixon.

Q. In 1872 what Davenport native became the nation's first woman high school principal?

A. Phoebe Sudlow.

Q. Where was the first Quaker church west of the Mississippi River founded?

A. Salem.

Q. The administration building for the University of Iowa was originally used for what purpose?

A. State capitol.

Q. Potter's Mill, the state's oldest grist mill, is situated in what town?

A. Bellevue.

Q. After graduating from West Point in 1828, what Civil War figure operated a sawmill on the Yellow River while serving in the U.S. Army at Fort Crawford?

A. Jefferson Davis.

Q. Ten kids from what high school were the mock-trial national champions in 2001?

A. Pocahontas.

Q. Astronaut David Hilmer, actor James Daly, and author Marjorie Holmes are alumni of what college?

A. Cornell College, in Mount Vernon.

Q. Who was the first native Iowan to be state governor?

A. Beryl F. Carroll (1909–13) from Bloomfield.

Q. The world's oldest lawyer, Cornelius Van de Steeg of Perry, practiced his profession up to what age?

A. 101 years, 11 months.

————◆————

Q. In what year did the Electric Interurban (a trolley) begin running between Mason City and Clear Lake on a regular time schedule?

A. 1897 (the only one in the U.S. that has survived).

————◆————

Q. Who was the only Iowa governor to serve two non-consecutive terms?

A. Samuel J. Kirkwood (1860–64 and 1876–77).

————◆————

Q. In 1876 the Des Moines police force was established with how many men?

A. Eight.

————◆————

Q. Because of scarcity of timber, what substitute material was used for many pioneer homes in northwest Iowa?

A. Sod.

————◆————

Q. In what year was the state constitution changed to increase the governor's term from two to four years?

A. 1972.

————◆————

Q. For what is the Reverend John Todd House in Tabor famous?

A. It was a major station on the Underground Railroad.

Q. For what Glidden native was the B-29 that dropped the atomic bomb on Hiroshima named?

A. Enola Gay Haggard (mother of the pilot, Col. Paul W. Tibbets).

Q. What was the name of a colony settled in Decatur County in 1859 by a group of Hungarians?

A. New Buda.

Q. Who is the only Iowan to serve as U.S. Speaker of the House?

A. David B. Henderson.

Q. When was the first fatal automobile accident in Iowa (a Hampton man struck a bridge)?

A. September 29, 1905.

Q. The Harrison County Historical Village opened as a museum in 1938 and was known for serving a free sample of what?

A. Cherry drink (they still serve it).

Q. What year did the unsolved Villisca axe murders take place in which eight people were killed?

A. 1912.

Q. Of whom did Gen. Ulysses S. Grant say, "No soldier on the firing line gave more heroic service than she rendered"?

A. Annie Wittenmyer (a wealthy Keokuk matron).

Q. In 1942 an ordnance plant employing nineteen thousand workers was opened by the federal government in what city to manufacture ammunition?

A. Ankeny.

Q. What Iowa governor was in Ford's Theater with Abraham Lincoln when Lincoln was shot?

A. William Milo Stone.

Q. What type of factory did Governor Lee Elthon successfully operate in Fertile when he was thirty-three?

A. Dill pickle.

Q. What denomination built the first church in Iowa in 1834 in Dubuque?

A. Methodist.

Q. What is the only school in the nation to have its entire campus listed in the *National Register of Historic Places*?

A. Cornell College.

Q. What Dexter native was U.S. ambassador to China, Brazil, and Mexico?

A. Edwin H. Conger.

Q. What sandwich did Muscatine butcher Fred Angell create in 1926?

A. Maid Rite.

Q. In 1868 the first law school west of the Mississippi moved to the University of Iowa after being established three years earlier in what town?

A. Des Moines.

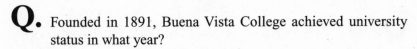

Q. In what year did Des Moines become the second city in the nation to have kindergarten as a part of its public school system?

A. 1884.

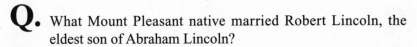

Q. Founded in 1891, Buena Vista College achieved university status in what year?

A. 1995.

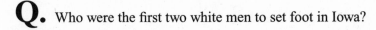

Q. What Mount Pleasant native married Robert Lincoln, the eldest son of Abraham Lincoln?

A. Mary Harlan.

Q. Who were the first two white men to set foot in Iowa?

A. Louis Jolliet and Father Jacques Marquette.

Q. Ames was known by what name until 1866?

A. College Farm.

Q. Where did the word *tractor* originate?

A. Charles City.

Q. Serving from 1923 to 1924, R. W. Cassaday was the first woman to hold what state office?

A. Secretary of agriculture.

Q. In what year was the University of Iowa founded?

A. 1847.

Q. How much salary did Herbert Hoover receive as president?

A. None (he wouldn't accept any).

Q. Who was a barber in Creston from 1895–1903 and founded a petroleum company in Oklahoma in 1917?

A. Frank Phillips.

Q. What son of a famous frontiersman founded Oskaloosa?

A. Capt. Nathan Boone (son of Daniel Boone).

Q. In what year was the first telegraphic message sent in Iowa?

A. 1848.

Q. Iowa began its tradition of holding the nation's earliest presidential caucuses in what year?

A. 1972.

Q. Opened on the north side of Forest City in 1898, what hotel was decorated in black?

A. The Summit.

Q. Opened on the south side of Forest City in 1899, what hotel was decorated in white?

A. The Waldorf.

———◆———

Q. What Burlington man *suggested* that Iowans call themselves Hawkeyes?

A. Judge David Rorer.

———◆———

Q. In 1946 what Postville native won the Nobel Peace Prize for his YMCA work and for aiding displaced persons?

A. John Mott.

———◆———

Q. In what hamlet did former governor William Larrabee and his wife establish a school as their gift to the people?

A. Clermont.

———◆———

Q. In 1918 where was Iowa's first public junior college established?

A. Mason City.

———◆———

Q. What type of company did W. A. Sheaffer establish in Fort Madison in 1913?

A. Fountain pen company.

———◆———

Q. Who was Iowa's last territorial governor?

A. James Clarke.

Q. Where was the Republican Party first organized in Iowa?

A. Crawfordsville.

———◆———

Q. How many Iowa counties are named after U.S. presidents?

A. Eleven (Adams, Buchanan, Harrison, Jackson, Jefferson, Madison, Monroe, Polk, Taylor, Van Buren, and Washington).

———◆———

Q. What was the first public university in the nation to admit men and women on an equal basis?

A. University of Iowa.

———◆———

Q. What Knoxville resident designed the Iowa state flag?

A. Dixie Cornell Gebhardt.

———◆———

Q. Bancroft's Greenwood Cemetery is the final resting place of Rev. Ozias A. Littlefield, the founder of what church?

A. The Little Brown Church.

———◆———

Q. What percentage of Iowa's schools rank above the national average in scholastic achievement?

A. 93 percent.

———◆———

Q. In what year was "Fort" dropped from the Des Moines city name?

A. 1857.

Q. What duo robbed the Knierim bank of $272 in 1934?

A. Bonnie Parker and Clyde Barrow.

———◆———

Q. For how many years did James Wilson serve as the U.S. secretary of agriculture?

A. Sixteen.

———◆———

Q. What bells in Jefferson chime every quarter-hour?

A. The Mahanay Memorial Carillon.

———◆———

Q. Waldorf College alumnus John K. Hanson was founder and chairman of the board of what *Fortune* 500 company?

A. Winnebago Industries.

———◆———

Q. What product was harvested from the Iowa Great Lakes from the 1880s until the 1950s, generating a substantial business?

A. Ice.

———◆———

Q. The first religious services in George were held in what structure?

A. Train depot.

———◆———

Q. What is the name of the free student-operated bus system at the University of Iowa?

A. Cambus.

Q. The only pair of brothers to serve in the state legislature from the same county at the same time had what surname?

A. Lynes.

———◆———

Q. Who was the first teacher in Clear Lake, later a victim in the Spirit Lake Massacre?

A. Eliza Gardner.

———◆———

Q. What Monroe County town, with a population of about six thousand in 1910, was composed mostly of African Americans?

A. Buxton.

———◆———

Q. When the first post office was built in Des Moines in 1850, who was appointed postmaster?

A. Hoyt Sherman.

———◆———

Q. The Iowa income tax on individuals was enacted by the legislature in what year?

A. 1934.

———◆———

Q. The northernmost Confederate raid of the Civil War occurred in what county?

A. Davis.

———◆———

Q. In 1943 what wholly new crop were Iowa farmers asked to grow sixty thousand acres of to help the war effort?

A. Hemp.

Q. What was the name of the short-lived colony founded by Abner Kneeland in the late 1830s in Van Buren County, whose inhabitants did not believe in God or religion?

A. Salubria.

Q. At what institution did the first public university school of religion begin?

A. University of Iowa.

Q. Who was described as "the Finest Orator in Congress" after addressing the House of Representatives concerning aid for families of sailors who died in the sinking of the *Maine*?

A. Robert Gordon Cousins.

Q. What college in Epworth is the nation's only four-year Catholic seminary devoted exclusively to training young men for foreign missions?

A. Divine Word College.

Q. As of 2000 what was the population of Iowa?

A. 2.9 million.

Q. What are the five telephone area codes for Iowa?

A. 319, 515, 563, 641, and 712.

Q. In what year was the first railroad bridge built across the Mississippi River?

A. 1856.

Q. Abbot Bruno laid the foundation of what Trappist monastery near Dubuque in 1849?

A. New Melleray.

Q. As head of the WPA, what Sioux City native spent more than $9 billion during the depression of the 1930s?

A. Harry Hopkins.

Q. What sandwich is claimed to have been devised by Clarinda restaurant owner Bert Gray and named by his chef, who was from Germany?

A. Hamburger.

Q. In what year did a driver's license become mandatory for all drivers in Iowa?

A. 1932.

Q. The land that became the state of Iowa was acquired during whose presidency?

A. Thomas Jefferson.

Q. In what year was an electric motor first added to a Maytag washer?

A. 1911.

Q. A display of dolls in the state capitol represents whom?

A. The first ladies of Iowa.

Q. What Iowan was secretary of war under President U. S. Grant in 1869?

A. William W. Belknap.

Q. The grave of what Native American chief is in downtown Sioux City?

A. War Eagle.

Q. How many state universities are in Iowa?

A. Three (Iowa State University, University of Iowa, and University of Northern Iowa).

Q. With an average age of fifty-seven, what was the nickname of the Thirty-seventh Iowa Infantry Regiment that was mustered into the Union army on December 15, 1862?

A. The Graybeard Regiment.

Q. For how many years did the state have no senators in Washington, D.C.?

A. Two (from late 1846 and into 1848).

Q. In 1908 the first women's suffrage parade was held in what town?

A. Boone.

Q. In what year did the Amana colonists arrive in Iowa?

A. 1854.

Q. With what religious denomination was Central College affiliated when it opened in 1853?

A. Baptist.

Q. What two men started the Quaker Oats Company in 1873?

A. George W. Douglas and Robert Stuart.

Q. The term *Reynards,* which the French called the Mesquakie Indians, has what meaning?

A. Foxes.

Q. President Franklin Roosevelt and his Republican challenger Alf Landon met in Des Moines on September 3, 1936, to attend what event?

A. The National Drought Conference.

Q. Since October 1976, what has been the name of the official governor's residence?

A. Terrace Hill.

Q. How many federal defense installations are in the state?

A. None.

Q. When it was completed in the 1920s, what was the name of the first paved, transcontinental highway which crossed Iowa?

A. The Lincoln Highway.

Q. Who was Iowa's first white settler?

A. Julien Dubuque.

———◆———

Q. Where was the state's first public library established in 1853?

A. Fairfield.

———◆———

Q. What job did Richard W. Sears, founder of Sears and Roebuck, hold while a resident of Lake Mills?

A. Railroad depot agent.

———◆———

Q. What college has the oldest undergraduate social work degree program in Iowa?

A. Wartburg.

———◆———

Q. What Afton man and graduate of Creston High School ran the White House as assistant and chief usher under six presidents?

A. James Bernard "J. B." West (asst. 1941–57; chief 1957–1969).

———◆———

Q. Jessie F. Binford was born in Marshalltown and is a member of the Iowa Women's Hall of Fame for giving her life to help the less fortunate people of what city?

A. Chicago.

———◆———

Q. What county has the oldest county library system in the state?

A. Scott.

Q. In 1882 Des Moines paved some downtown streets with what unusual material?

A. Cedar blocks.

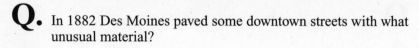

Q. In 1985 the one-hundred-year-old Bankers Life Company changed its name to what?

A. Principal Financial Group.

Q. What Iowa governor served five terms?

A. Robert Ray.

Q. Families from what country were the first white settlers in Lyon County, settling near the Big Sioux River?

A. Norway.

Q. Salveson Hall of Waldorf College was erected as what building?

A. The Waldorf Hotel.

Q. The Kinsman Monument in Council Bluffs honors veterans of what war?

A. The Civil War.

Q. The first woman to hold a county courthouse job, Emily Stebbins, was appointed deputy recorder and treasurer of Chickasaw County in what year?

A. 1862.

Q. Who was the first governor of the territory of Iowa?

A. Robert Lucas.

◆

Q. Who was the only member of the Lewis and Clark expedition to die during the three-year journey?

A. Sgt. Charles Floyd (who was buried near Sioux City).

◆

Q. What two Iowans have been appointed to the U.S. Supreme Court?

A. Samuel F. Miller and Wiley B. Rutledge.

◆

Q. The oldest college in the state, what private four-year liberal arts college was founded in 1839 by Dubuque's first Catholic bishop?

A. Loras College.

◆

Q. What do the insurance company initials IMT represent?

A. Iowa Mutual Tornado.

◆

Q. What steamboat that sank in the Missouri River in 1866 was raised from the mud in 1965 with much of its cargo preserved?

A. The *Bertrand.*

◆

Q. Because its laborers were paid in groceries and dry goods, what was another name for the failed Lyons-Iowa Central Railroad?

A. Calico Road.

Q. What Bloomfield lawyer was a Civil War brigadier general, editor of the *Davis County Republican,* and twice a candidate for the U.S. presidency?

A. James B. Weaver.

──────◆──────

Q. At the turn of the century, what college with just thirteen students decided to expand rather than close, and by 1907 had a new campus complete with a college of liberal arts?

A. University of Dubuque.

──────◆──────

Q. The first elevated railroad in the West, a prototype of Chicago's "El," was erected in what city in 1891?

A. Sioux City.

──────◆──────

Q. Where was Iowa's first fire department organized?

A. Carroll.

──────◆──────

Q. With bank deposits totaling over half a million dollars—amounting to $971 for every man, woman, and child in the town—what town claimed to be the nation's richest in 1915?

A. Walker.

──────◆──────

Q. What Iowan became secretary of the interior in 1881 under James Garfield?

A. Samuel J. Kirkwood.

──────◆──────

Q. In what year did Iowa become a territory?

A. 1838.

Q. Where is the birthplace of Mamie Doud Eisenhower?

A. Boone.

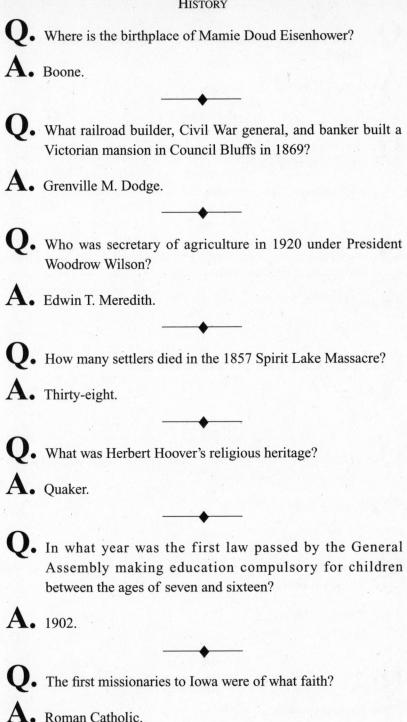

Q. What railroad builder, Civil War general, and banker built a Victorian mansion in Council Bluffs in 1869?

A. Grenville M. Dodge.

Q. Who was secretary of agriculture in 1920 under President Woodrow Wilson?

A. Edwin T. Meredith.

Q. How many settlers died in the 1857 Spirit Lake Massacre?

A. Thirty-eight.

Q. What was Herbert Hoover's religious heritage?

A. Quaker.

Q. In what year was the first law passed by the General Assembly making education compulsory for children between the ages of seven and sixteen?

A. 1902.

Q. The first missionaries to Iowa were of what faith?

A. Roman Catholic.

Q. Who was the youngest man ever elected governor of the state?

A. Terry Branstad.

———◆———

Q. By what decade were more Iowans living in cities than in small towns or farms?

A. The 1960s.

———◆———

Q. In what year was the Rural Free Delivery Act passed establishing mail delivery to Iowa farms?

A. 1896.

———◆———

Q. How many domes are on the state capitol?

A. Five.

———◆———

Q. In 1913 what was the first great hydroelectric project completed in the United States?

A. Keokuk Dam.

———◆———

Q. Who was the first occupant of the present governor's offices in the capitol?

A. Buren R. Sherman.

———◆———

Q. What is the largest single religious denomination in Iowa?

A. Roman Catholic.

Q. In what year was the Danish Windmill shipped to Elk Horn and rebuilt by community volunteers?

A. 1976.

Q. Approximately how many weddings are held annually at the Little Brown Church in the Vale?

A. 625.

Q. Having organized her own military company for girls, Company G, who was the only woman to graduate from Iowa State College in 1880?

A. Carrie Lane Chapman Catt.

Q. The University of Northern Iowa, previously known as the State College of Iowa and Iowa State Teachers College, was founded in 1876 with what name?

A. Iowa State Normal School.

Q. Who established Iowa's first lending library with his personal collection of more than four hundred books?

A. Elbridge Gerry Potter.

Q. For a few weeks in 1926, all banks in what city failed, making it the largest city in the nation without a bank?

A. Jefferson.

Q. In what year did Cornell College become the first U.S. college to elevate a woman to full professorship with a salary equal to her male colleagues?

A. 1871.

Q. The Mormon Battalion's two-thousand-mile infantry march, the longest one known, began in Council Bluffs in July 1846 and ended six months later in San Diego for service in what war?

A. The Mexican War.

◆

Q. What college in Fairfield opened in 1875 and closed in 1973?

A. Parsons.

◆

Q. What Ida Grove native was elected governor three times and became a U.S. senator in 1968?

A. Harold Hughes.

◆

Q. Where can you find the profile of Indian Chief Tall Tree, who helped build peaceful relations with settlers in Page County?

A. The U.S. nickel.

◆

Q. In what year did thirteen hundred European Mormon converts carry their possessions from Iowa City to Salt Lake City in handcarts?

A. 1856.

◆

Q. Before being designated U.S. Highway 65 in 1965, the road that runs two thousand miles from New Orleans to Winnipeg, across Iowa, was known by what name?

A. The Pine to Palm Highway (also the Jefferson Highway).

◆

Q. DeWitt, selected as the Clinton County seat in 1841, was formerly known by what name?

A. Vanderburg.

Q. Built in 1886, where is the oldest Lutheran church in continuous use west of the Mississippi?

A. St. Ansgar (First Lutheran Norwegian Church).

◆

Q. The use of what Davenport college facilities by the navy during World War II kept that school alive and its faculty employed?

A. Saint Ambrose.

◆

Q. Who was Iowa's governor during the Civil War?

A. Samuel J. Kirkwood.

◆

Q. Due to lack of timber, the first settlers in Osceola County were urged to plant what to use as fuel?

A. Sunflowers (an acre yielded burning material equal to six cords of good dry wood).

◆

Q. Maker of printing presses and avionics equipment, what company is the largest employer in Cedar Rapids?

A. Rockwell International.

◆

Q. What Iowan was secretary of agriculture under Presidents William McKinley, Theodore Roosevelt, and William Howard Taft?

A. James Wilson.

◆

Q. What do the four *H*s of the 4-H symbol stand for?

A. Head, heart, hands, and health.

Q. In what year did the Mormons begin their trek across Iowa?

A. 1846.

Q. Who were Iowa's first two senators?

A. George W. Jones and Augustus Caesar Dodge.

Q. What Native American tribe is thought to be the only one to cede land to Americans and then buy back part of it for a permanent home?

A. Mesquakie.

Q. In what year did a new state law give all children the right to free high school tuition?

A. 1911.

Q. Tom Vilsack became the first Democrat to be elected governor (1998) in how many years?

A. Thirty-six (since Harold Hughes).

Q. What Waverly woman was the first female to run for public office in Iowa?

A. May E. Francis, who in 1922 ran for superintendent of public instruction.

Q. At what naval air station was Richard M. Nixon stationed in 1942 and 1943?

A. Ottumwa.

Q. What university was founded in the early 1970s as an expression of area pride and is acclaimed as a mythical "University of the Mind"?

A. University of Okoboji.

Q. In what year was Iowa's Historical Department established?

A. 1892.

Q. Who was governor of Iowa from 1943 to 1945 and U.S. senator from 1945 to 1968?

A. Bourke Hickenlooper.

Q. What thirteen-year-old girl was captured by a band of Sioux during the Spirit Lake Massacre of 1857?

A. Abigail Gardner.

Q. For the first time ever, three heads of state met in Iowa on October 21, 1995, representing what three countries?

A. United States, Czech Republic, and Republic of Slovakia.

Q. At the turn of the century, what city was known as "the Cigar-making Capital of the Midwest"?

A. Davenport.

Q. What county was named for a major who was killed in the Mexican War?

A. Ringgold.

Q. Iowa's first governor was inaugurated how many days before President James K. Polk signed the bill of admission bringing the state into existence?

A. Twenty-five (the bill of admission was signed December 28, 1846).

Q. What general from Mason City was wounded in both world wars and from 1925 to 1928 was Dwight Eisenhower's boss as assistant secretary of war?

A. Hanford MacNider.

Q. Who served as an Iowa senator at the same time his father served as a Wisconsin senator, marking the only time father and son have represented different states in the Senate simultaneously?

A. Augustus Caesar Dodge (Henry Dodge was his father).

Q. What president chose Council Bluffs as the eastern junction of the first transcontinental railroad?

A. Abraham Lincoln.

Q. In what year was the state capital moved from Iowa City to Des Moines?

A. 1857.

Q. Who built Terrace Hill in Des Moines in 1869?

A. Benjamin Franklin Allen.

Q. Lyman Dillon plowed a furrow how many miles long from Dubuque to Iowa City?

A. One hundred.

Q. When Iowa's first school, a log cabin built by Dr. Isaac Galland, opened in 1830 in Lee County, what was the teacher's pay?

A. Permission to read Dr. Galland's medical books.

———◆———

Q. From the laying of the first cornerstone in 1871 until the Supreme Court room was dedicated in 1886, the total cost of the state capitol was $2,873,294.59, with what amount being unaccounted for?

A. $3.77.

———◆———

Q. The Morgan Manor Hunting Lodge of Massena, built in 1887, is celebrated locally for being used as what during WW II?

A. An obstetric hospital (all 212 babies delivered there survived).

———◆———

Q. What was built on the spot where Pope John Paul II gave an address and held a worship service in 1979?

A. The Church of the Land.

———◆———

Q. A monument to Sgt. Charles Floyd was registered as the first National Historic Landmark by the U.S. Department of the Interior in what year?

A. 1960.

———◆———

Q. In 1858 what college became the first in Iowa to confer a baccalaureate degree on a woman?

A. Cornell.

———◆———

Q. What was the original name of the Franklin County seat of Hampton?

A. Benjamin.

Q. What ill Iowa senator had to be carried into the U.S. Senate chambers in order to vote "not guilty" on President Andrew Johnson's impeachment?

A. James W. Grimes.

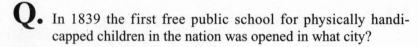

Q. What Union officer from Burlington inspired the cry "Hold the fort" during a battle at Alatoona, Georgia, in 1864?

A. John M. Corse.

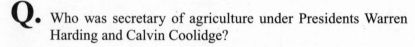

Q. In 1839 the first free public school for physically handicapped children in the nation was opened in what city?

A. Des Moines.

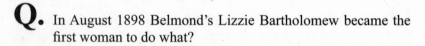

Q. Who was secretary of agriculture under Presidents Warren Harding and Calvin Coolidge?

A. Henry C. Wallace (father of Henry A. Wallace).

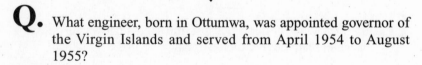

Q. In August 1898 Belmond's Lizzie Bartholomew became the first woman to do what?

A. Be licensed as a funeral director.

Q. What engineer, born in Ottumwa, was appointed governor of the Virgin Islands and served from April 1954 to August 1955?

A. Archie Alexander.

Q. What was Buffalo Bill's real name?

A. William Frederick Cody.

ARTS & LITERATURE

CHAPTER FOUR

Q. What composer was born in Oskaloosa and known as "America's Waltz King"?

A. Frederick Knight Logan.

Q. What Anamosa-born artist painted many of his works while he was a professor at the University of Iowa?

A. Grant Wood (1891–1942).

Q. What town library contains the Mark Twain Center?

A. Keokuk.

Q. What author was born in Storm Lake on May 21, 1944?

A. Janet Dailey.

Q. As of 2001 how many Pulitzer Prizes had been won by staff members of the *Des Moines Register*?

A. Fifteen.

Q. What CBS news broadcaster and *60 Minutes* reporter was born in Dakota City in 1923?

A. Harry Reasoner (1923–91).

———◆———

Q. James Stevens of Moravia published what book of fantastic tales in 1925?

A. *Paul Bunyan.*

———◆———

Q. Considered to be the father of the skyscraper, what architect designed Clinton's Van Allen Building?

A. Louis Sullivan.

———◆———

Q. What was the state's first newspaper?

A. *The Du Buque Visitor.*

———◆———

Q. What magazine was established by Henry Wallace and his son Henry C. Wallace in Des Moines in 1895?

A. *Wallace's Farmer.*

———◆———

Q. Council Bluffs's bronze sculpture *The Black Angel* is a memorial to whom?

A. Ruth Ann Dodge.

———◆———

Q. Iowans read more books per capita than how many other states?

A. Forty-nine.

Q. As of January 2001 how many Rhodes scholars had the University of Iowa produced?

A. Eighteen.

———◆———

Q. What Davenport native, who won a 1931 Pulitzer Prize for the play *Allison's House,* with her husband founded the Provincetown Players and "discovered" Eugene O'Neill?

A. Susan Glaspell (1882–1948).

———◆———

Q. Who was the first woman to receive a journalism master's degree from the University of Iowa?

A. Mildred Wirt (Benson) from Ladora.

———◆———

Q. What museum contains a collection of puppets and marionettes collected by puppeteer Bill Baird?

A. Charles H. MacNider Museum.

———◆———

Q. For more than thirty-five years, Riverside World, Inc. in Iowa Falls has been the world's largest distributor of what product?

A. Bibles.

———◆———

Q. What publication installed the world's first all-electronic newsroom?

A. The *Quad-City Times.*

———◆———

Q. Pella's annual celebration, Tulip Time, began in 1935 as an operetta produced by whom?

A. Pella High School students.

Q. What town is named after a Connecticut poet?

A. Sigourney (Lydia Huntley Sigourney).

———◆———

Q. What Colfax native moved to Tahiti and cowrote *Mutiny on the Bounty* with Charles Bernard Nordhoff?

A. James Norman Hall (1887–1951).

———◆———

Q. What major American author's grandparents, Ernest and Caroline Hancock Hall, lived near Dyersville more than 130 years ago?

A. Ernest Hemingway.

———◆———

Q. What Iowa City author is the creator of the character Rambo?

A. David Morrell.

———◆———

Q. What Clinton native established the University of Iowa's department of political science, the Historical Society's *Palimpsest,* and the *Iowa Journal of History*?

A. Benjamin "Mr. History of Iowa" Shambaugh.

———◆———

Q. Who shapes the butter sculptures at the Iowa State Fair?

A. Duffy Lyon.

———◆———

Q. What Grundy County native wrote the novels *Vandemark's Folly, The Hawkeye,* and *The Invisible Woman*?

A. Herbert Quick (1861–1925).

Q. Where is the world's largest collection of hand-carved chains, featuring eighty-three types of wood?

A. Monona Historical Museum.

━━━━━◆━━━━━

Q. Wartburg College is the only private college in Iowa to offer a major in what kind of therapy?

A. Music.

━━━━━◆━━━━━

Q. In what town did author Paul Hutchins, writer of the *Sugar Creek Gang* series, sit in his car in the driveway of the Evergreen Lawn Cemetery to write?

A. George.

━━━━━◆━━━━━

Q. What Cedar Falls native wrote the novel *A Lantern in Her Hand*?

A. Bess Streeter Aldrich (1881–1954).

━━━━━◆━━━━━

Q. What Iowa State University graduate and Associated Press correspondent was kidnapped in Beirut on March 16, 1985?

A. Terry Anderson.

━━━━━◆━━━━━

Q. From what high school and college did the New York Metropolitan Opera baritone Simon Estes graduate?

A. Centerville High School, and the University of Iowa School of Music.

━━━━━◆━━━━━

Q. What Davenport author wrote *Stories of A Western Town* (1893) and *Man of the Hour* (1905) under the pen name Octave Thanet?

A. Alice French (1850–1934).

Q. What Ottumwa native has investigated UFOs for the government and written books on the subject?

A. Donald Keyhoe.

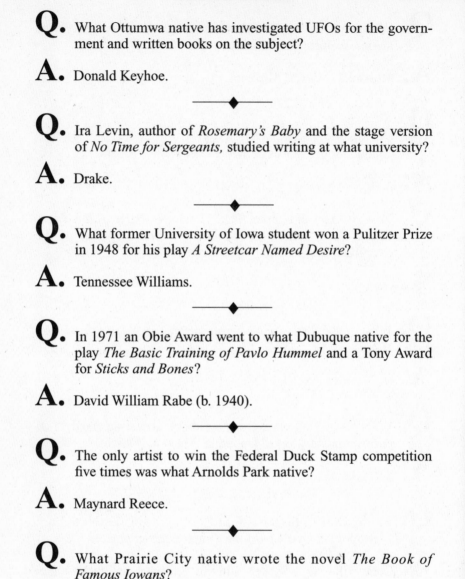

Q. Ira Levin, author of *Rosemary's Baby* and the stage version of *No Time for Sergeants,* studied writing at what university?

A. Drake.

Q. What former University of Iowa student won a Pulitzer Prize in 1948 for his play *A Streetcar Named Desire*?

A. Tennessee Williams.

Q. In 1971 an Obie Award went to what Dubuque native for the play *The Basic Training of Pavlo Hummel* and a Tony Award for *Sticks and Bones*?

A. David William Rabe (b. 1940).

Q. The only artist to win the Federal Duck Stamp competition five times was what Arnolds Park native?

A. Maynard Reece.

Q. What Prairie City native wrote the novel *The Book of Famous Iowans*?

A. Douglas Bauer.

Q. What Keosauqua native and novelist saw his books *One Destiny* and *State Fair* turned into films?

A. Phil Stong (1899–1957).

Q. Where was Robert James Waller, author of *The Bridges of Madison County,* born?

A. Rockford.

Q. During the 1920s, what writer from Cedar Rapids was famous for the satires he wrote about New Yorkers?

A. Carl Van Vechten (1880–1964).

Q. The Salisbury House in Des Moines is a replica of King's House in what English town?

A. Salisbury.

Q. University of Iowa alumnus Mildred Wirt Benson was the creator of what mystery series for young people?

A. *Nancy Drew.*

Q. An Iowa town and county were both named for what Swedish novelist?

A. Bremer (Frederika).

Q. What city does the Des Moines Metro Opera call home?

A. Indianola.

Q. What Fort Dodge native became a nun and designed the first U.S. LOVE stamp?

A. Mary Corita Kent (Sister Mary Corita, 1918–86).

Q. With what city are authors Richard Bach *(Jonathan Livingston Seagull)* and Edna Ferber *(Giant)* associated?

A. Ottumwa.

Q. The 1914 Brenton National Bank building in Grinnell was one of the last structures designed by what famous architect?

A. Louis Sullivan.

Q. Who sculpted the *Chief Wapello* statue at the courthouse in Ottumwa?

A. Nellie Verne Walker.

Q. The first written reference to *Iowa* was in the title of a book written by whom?

A. Albert M. Lea *(Notes on the Wisconsin Territory; Particularly with Reference to the Iowa District, or Black Hawk Purchase).*

Q. In what year did the annual North Iowa Band Festival begin?

A. 1936.

Q. What type of palace was used to advertise the fertile fields of southwest Iowa from 1889 to 1892?

A. Bluegrass.

Q. For what novel did Iowa resident Edna Ferber (1887–1968) win a 1925 Pulitzer Prize?

A. *So Big.*

Q. What circus composer and musician lived in Fort Dodge from 1919 until his death in 1971?

A. Karl King.

———◆———

Q. For what book did Keokuk's Cornelia Meigs win the 1934 Newbery Medal for distinguished contribution to American literature for children?

A. *Invincible Louisa.*

———◆———

Q. What was the occupation of the father of sculptor Nellie Verne Walker, who was born in Red Oak, grew up in Moulton, and was influenced by his work?

A. Tombstone maker.

———◆———

Q. What writer, born near Le Mars in 1927, tells about his early years in Iowa in his book *We Have All Gone Away*?

A. Curtis Harnack.

———◆———

Q. What is the state song?

A. "The Song of Iowa."

———◆———

Q. What Lyons native won the 1970 Pulitzer Prize in journalism for commentary and wrote *Mighty Mississippi: Biography of a River* in 1982?

A. Marquis Childs.

———◆———

Q. What author and her family lived from 1876 to 1877 in a hotel in Burr Oak?

A. Laura Ingalls Wilder (1867–1957).

Q. Who designed six homes in Mason City from 1912–17 and the capitol of Australia?

A. Walter Burley Griffin.

------◆------

Q. Grant Wood designed nine murals depicting phases of agriculture for what building at Iowa State College?

A. The library.

------◆------

Q. As of 2001 the University of Iowa had produced how many Pulitzer Prize winners?

A. Thirteen (Jorie Graham, in 1996, for poetry, was the most recent).

------◆------

Q. What was the birthplace of the art calendar industry in 1888?

A. Red Oak.

------◆------

Q. What author, born in Storm Lake, is known for her spiritual writing and such novels as *Three from Galilee* and *The Messiah*?

A. Marjorie Holmes.

------◆------

Q. Iowa State University faculty members Lee Hadley and Ann Irwin cowrote ten novels for young adults under what pseudonym?

A. Hadley Irwin.

------◆------

Q. What Cedar Rapids poet established the International Writing Program and served as director of the renowned Iowa Writers' Workshop at the University of Iowa?

A. Paul Engle (d. 1991).

Q. While learning her craft in Earlville, what writer kept bees for a living?

A. Ruth Sukow (1892–1960).

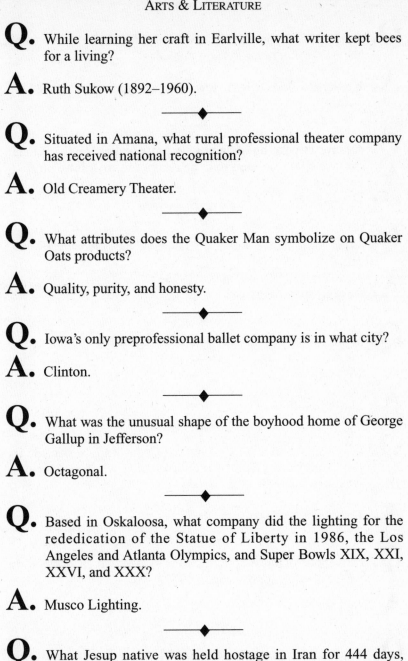

Q. Situated in Amana, what rural professional theater company has received national recognition?

A. Old Creamery Theater.

Q. What attributes does the Quaker Man symbolize on Quaker Oats products?

A. Quality, purity, and honesty.

Q. Iowa's only preprofessional ballet company is in what city?

A. Clinton.

Q. What was the unusual shape of the boyhood home of George Gallup in Jefferson?

A. Octagonal.

Q. Based in Oskaloosa, what company did the lighting for the rededication of the Statue of Liberty in 1986, the Los Angeles and Atlanta Olympics, and Super Bowls XIX, XXI, XXVI, and XXX?

A. Musco Lighting.

Q. What Jesup native was held hostage in Iran for 444 days, then returned home in 1981 to write the book *Guest of the Revolution*?

A. Kathryn Koob.

Q. Since 1969, where is the nation's oldest literary magazine, the *North American Review,* published?

A. University of Northern Iowa (began publication in 1815 in Boston).

------◆------

Q. Before becoming an actor or politician, Ronald Reagan wrote a sports column for a newspaper in what Iowa city?

A. Des Moines.

------◆------

Q. What Pella native was a publisher of the *Saturday Evening Post*?

A. Cory Synhorst Servass.

------◆------

Q. What Sioux City native, who grew up in Mason City, wrote the books *No Greener Meadows* and *The Girl in the Spike-Heeled Shoes*?

A. Martin Yoseloff.

------◆------

Q. Carl Van Vechten (1880–1964) of Cedar Rapids, became the first American critic of modern dance while working for what newspaper?

A. The *New York Times*.

------◆------

Q. University of Iowa alumnus Max A. Collins Jr. became the writer of what comic strip in 1977?

A. *Dick Tracy.*

------◆------

Q. The 30,000-square-foot complex dedicated to the life of Mason City's Meredith Wilson is called what?

A. Music Man Square (dedication set for 2002, Wilson's 100th birthday).

Q. What magazine did Des Moines' Meredith Publishing Company start publishing in 1922?

A. *Better Homes and Gardens.*

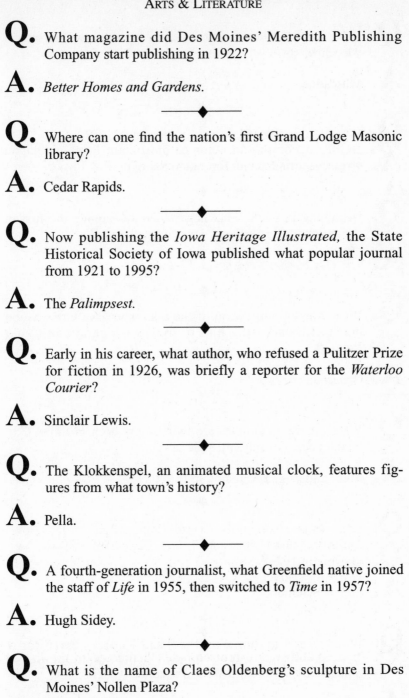

Q. Where can one find the nation's first Grand Lodge Masonic library?

A. Cedar Rapids.

Q. Now publishing the *Iowa Heritage Illustrated,* the State Historical Society of Iowa published what popular journal from 1921 to 1995?

A. The *Palimpsest.*

Q. Early in his career, what author, who refused a Pulitzer Prize for fiction in 1926, was briefly a reporter for the *Waterloo Courier*?

A. Sinclair Lewis.

Q. The Klokkenspel, an animated musical clock, features figures from what town's history?

A. Pella.

Q. A fourth-generation journalist, what Greenfield native joined the staff of *Life* in 1955, then switched to *Time* in 1957?

A. Hugh Sidey.

Q. What is the name of Claes Oldenberg's sculpture in Des Moines' Nollen Plaza?

A. *The Crusoe Umbrella.*

Q. Mark Twain, a temporary resident, believed the sunsets in what Iowa town were without equal?

A. Muscatine.

Q. What percentage of Iowans can read and write?

A. 99 percent (highest in the United States).

Q. Beginning in 1928, what newspaper was among the first in the nation to use airplanes for news gathering?

A. The *Des Moines Register and Tribune.*

Q. What was the profession of the man who gave Grant Wood his start by allowing him to live in his garage in Cedar Rapids?

A. Undertaker.

Q. What advice columnists are twin sisters born in Sioux City on the Fourth of July in 1918?

A. Ann Landers and Abigail Van Buren.

Q. What senior pastor at the Crystal Cathedral in Garden Grove, California, and host of television's *Hour of Power,* was born in Alton in 1926?

A. Robert Schuller.

Q. What Osage author won the 1922 Pulitzer Prize for *A Daughter of the Middle Border* in his autobiographical series?

A. Hamlin Garland.

Q. What is the name of the Edwin Blashfield mural in the Iowa Capitol, which depicts the pioneers?

A. Westward.

◆

Q. How much did the Art Institute of Chicago pay for Grant Wood's painting *American Gothic*?

A. Three hundred dollars.

◆

Q. Fort Dodge native Thomas Heggen wrote what novel that became a play and a film starring Henry Fonda?

A. *Mister Roberts.*

◆

Q. What Newton author, an advocate of conservation, was largely responsible for the passage of a congressional act to save the buffalo in Yellowstone National Park?

A. Emerson Hough (1857–1923).

◆

Q. What novel describing the horrors of a Confederate prison camp won Webster City native MacKinlay Kantor a 1955 Pulitzer Prize?

A. *Andersonville.*

◆

Q. Where is the Museum of Religious Arts?

A. Harrison County, between Logan and Missouri Valley.

◆

Q. Growing up in Bode, Gene Olson has written more than 140 books of science fiction and religion under what name?

A. Brad Steiger.

Q. In 1920 Cornell became the first academic institution to invite what poet to lecture and read his works?

A. Carl Sandburg.

———◆———

Q. The Iowa state capitol is an excellent example of what type of architecture?

A. Romanesque.

———◆———

Q. What Mason City native as editorial cartoonist for the *Denver Post* and the *Los Angeles Times* won three Pulitzer Prizes?

A. Paul Conrad.

———◆———

Q. Named at birth Roy Frowick, what New York fashion designer was born in Des Moines and attended Roosevelt High School there?

A. Roy Halston (b. 1932).

———◆———

Q. What Grammy- and Academy Award-winning jazz musician earned his bachelor of arts degree at Grinnell College?

A. Herbie Hancock.

———◆———

Q. What prolific author of such books as *Tales of the South Pacific, Centennial,* and *Hawaii* studied at the University of Iowa Writers' Workshop?

A. James A. Michener.

———◆———

Q. What is the third largest paid circulation magazine in the nation behind *T.V. Guide* and *Reader's Digest*?

A. *Better Homes and Gardens* (7.6 million).

Q. The 1972 Pulitzer Prize for fiction was won by what Lake Mills native for *Angle of Repose*?

A. Wallace Stegner.

Q. What Woodbury County native is the official portrait artist for Jimmy Carter and has drawn covers for *Time* magazine?

A. Robert Templeton.

Q. What Davenport native wrote the book *Old Ironsides* and was editor of the *World Almanac* from 1948 to 1965?

A. Harry Hansen.

Q. Who designed Cedar Rock, a home of Usonian architecture, in Quasqueton?

A. Frank Lloyd Wright.

Q. The Iowa State campus includes several sculptures by what artist-in-residence from 1937 to 1955?

A. Christian Petersen.

Q. What former Sheldon resident wrote the books *A Literary History of Iowa, Growing Up in Iowa,* and *Christmas in Iowa*?

A. Clarence Andrews.

Q. What Wiota farmer and postmaster became one of the most popular writers of dime novels in the late 1880s with such titles as *Hawkeye Harry* and *Tiger Tom, the Texas Terror*?

A. Oliver (Oll) Coomes.

Q. What Emmetsburg native was a managing editor of both the *New York Globe* and the *New Republic*?

A. Bruce Bliven.

Q. Who wrote *One Foot in Heaven,* a bestseller about a minister's life in fictionized Riverton (modeled after Burlington)?

A. Hartzell Spence (1908–2001, from Clarion).

Q. Spending the summer of 1893 in Spillville, what composer made final revisions of his *New World Symphony*?

A. Antonín Dvořák.

Q. Grant Wood established what artists' colony in 1932?

A. Stone City.

Q. At the height of his career, what *Des Moines Register* editorial cartoonist, syndicated through the *New York Tribune,* was enjoyed daily by millions of Americans?

A. Jay N. "Ding" Darling.

Q. The annual Rosemaling Exhibition is held in conjunction with what other festival?

A. Nordic Fest.

Q. Where was Honore Willsie Morrow, author of *With Malice Toward None* and *Mary Todd Lincoln,* born in 1880?

A. Ottumwa.

Q. What Montour native wrote biographies of Harry S. Truman, Lyndon Johnson, and Dwight D. Eisenhower?

A. Merle Miller (1919–86).

———◆———

Q. What Winterset native founded *Redbook* magazine?

A. Turnbull White.

———◆———

Q. Who composed "The Missouri Waltz"?

A. Frederick Knight Logan, an Iowa native.

———◆———

Q. Thomas O. Meredith of Meredith Publishing in Des Moines once built and operated a hotel in what town?

A. Marne.

———◆———

Q. How many different editions of the *Des Moines Register* are printed daily?

A. Three.

———◆———

Q. What is the state's oldest continuing newspaper?

A. The *Hawk Eye.*

———◆———

Q. While at the University of Iowa, W. P. Kinsella wrote the novel *Shoeless Joe,* which served as the basis for what movie?

A. *Field of Dreams.*

Q. What Cedar Rapids resident was instrumental in ushering in the golden era of the circuit Chautauqua (a literary/musical forum) in 1904?

A. Keith Vawter.

◆

Q. What Burnside native authored *Ballad to an Iowa Farmer and Other Reflections* and won a Pulitzer Prize for his national reporting on Jimmy Hoffa in 1958?

A. Clark Raymond Mollenhoff.

◆

Q. Who wrote "The Song of Iowa"?

A. Maj. S. H. M. Byers.

◆

Q. What was the first permanent art facility built in Iowa?

A. Blanden Memorial Art Museum in Fort Dodge.

◆

Q. In what town is the house that served as the backdrop in Grant Wood's painting *American Gothic*?

A. Eldon.

◆

Q. Where is Iowa's oldest continually running theater?

A. Story City.

◆

Q. What Adams County native founded and edited *Midland: A Magazine of the Middle West* from 1915 to 1933, and conducted the CBS radio program *Of Books and Men* in the 1930s and 1940s?

A. John T. Frederick.

Q. Although Harriet Ketcham of Mount Pleasant designed the Iowa Soldiers and Sailors Monument on the state capitol grounds, what sculptor completed the work?

A. Carl Rohl-Smith, after Ketcham's death.

Q. Where is Iowa's only operating antique carousel?

A. Story City.

Q. At the turn of the century, what Estherville man patented a process for painting theatrical scenery by using dye?

A. Jesse Cox.

Q. Who is Iowa's first poet laureate?

A. Marvin Bell (appointed to this honorary position in 2000).

Q. By 1905, with only 184 towns with a population of more than one thousand, Iowa had how many opera houses?

A. 122.

Q. What was the most unusual attraction at Ottumwa's Coal Palace in 1890 and 1891?

A. A miniature mine.

Q. What Iowa cartoonist was appointed head of the U.S. Biological Service by Franklin D. Roosevelt?

A. Jay N. "Ding" Darling.

Q. In what year did Iowa-based *Look* magazine cease publication?

A. 1971.

Q. The 1992 Pulitzer Prize for fiction went to what University of Iowa alumnus for *A Thousand Acres*?

A. Jane Smiley.

Q. What long-time *Chicago Daily News* drama critic was born in West Burlington and during the 1880s was famous as opera singer Lillie West?

A. Amy Leslie.

Q. What 1980 Pulitzer Prize–winning poet earned his doctorate at the University of Iowa in 1954?

A. Donald Justice.

Q. What county's courthouse is modeled after the Château Azay-le-Rideaux in the Loire Valley of France?

A. Dallas.

Q. Students and staff from Stephens College of Columbia, Missouri, put on professional plays each year at what theater?

A. Okoboji Summer Theatre.

Q. What architect designed a house for Dr. George C. Stockman in Mason City in 1908?

A. Frank Lloyd Wright.

Q. What well-known Iowan wrote such books as *Principles of Mining, American Individualism,* and *American Epic*?

A. Herbert Hoover.

Q. What Shenandoah native, a writer at the *Des Moines Register* from 1972–98, is known as "the Iowa Boy"?

A. Chuck Offenburger.

Q. Where is the world's largest collection of Grant Wood artwork?

A. Cedar Rapids Museum of Art.

Q. After it moved from Fort Madison in 1839, where is the *Hawk Eye* published today?

A. Burlington.

Q. What artist and illustrator, whose clients include *The New Yorker, Rolling Stone,* and *Cosmopolitan,* has his studio on Main Street in Cedar Falls?

A. Gary Kelley.

Q. In Phil Stong's 1932 classic novel *State Fair,* what was the name of Abel Frake's boar which claimed the Iowa State Fair Championship?

A. Blue Boy.

Q. What former director of the Iowa Historical Department, Museum and Archives Division, with his wife wrote *Waterfowl of Iowa,* which was illustrated by Maynard Reece?

A. Jack Musgrove.

Q. In a public expression of thanks for a bountiful harvest, what edifice was built in Sioux City in 1887?

A. A corn palace.

Q. What was the relationship between Grant Wood and the man who served as the model in *American Gothic*?

A. He was Wood's dentist.

Q. What 1935 novel by MacKinlay Kantor (1904–77) is the tale of a fox hunter's hound?

A. *The Voice of Bugle Ann.*

Q. A setting near Nashua was the inspiration for what hymn?

A. "The Church in the Wildwood."

Q. For how many years did Father Doberstein work alone and by hand on the Grotto of the Redemption?

A. Thirty-five (beginning in 1912; seven more years with help).

Q. What college hosts a Renaissance Faire each June?

A. Iowa Western Community College.

SPORTS & LEISURE

C H A P T E R   F I V E

Q. How long is RAGBRAI, the *Des Moines Register*'s Annual Great Bicycle Ride Across Iowa?

A. Five hundred miles.

---◆---

Q. Where are the Iowa Special Olympics summer games held?

A. Ames.

---◆---

Q. What town is home to Trainland USA?

A. Colfax.

---◆---

Q. What Baseball Hall of Famer, born in Sioux City, was described by Giants manager John McGraw as the best short-stop in baseball?

A. Dave "Beauty" Bancroft.

---◆---

Q. What is the hometown of fabled horseshoe pitcher Frank Jackson, who won the first world championship in 1909?

A. Kellerton (He went on to win six more championships).

Q. Each June, who do Readlyn residents crown as part of their annual celebration?

A. A grump.

◆

Q. Known as "the Hot-Air Ballooning Capital of the World," what town is home to the National Balloon Museum?

A. Indianola.

◆

Q. What Elberon native, who went on to play defensive lineman for the Dallas Cowboys, won the Outland Trophy while playing football for Air Force?

A. Chad Hennings.

◆

Q. Calling itself the Baseball Capital of Iowa, what community has won the most high school state baseball championships?

A. Norway.

◆

Q. What professional golfer from Davenport is the only Iowan to win the U.S. Open?

A. Jack Fleck.

◆

Q. Iowa City's Janet Guthrie became a professional in what sport?

A. Auto racing.

◆

Q. What undefeated world heavyweight champion professional wrestler was born in Iowa?

A. Frank Gotch.

Q. From 1985–89 Pomeroy-Palmer High School Boys won how many consecutive basketball games?

A. 103 (A state record).

Q. Who created the cornhusking contest, the first of which was held in December 1922 in Ankeny?

A. Henry A. Wallace.

Q. How long was the beard of Hans Langseth when he died in Kensett?

A. Seventeen feet, six inches.

Q. Who has won more Drake Relays championships than any other athlete in the meet's ninety-two-year history?

A. Kip Janvrin (from Panora, in the decathlon twelve times).

Q. When was the first state wrestling tournament held?

A. 1926.

Q. Who was the first African-American to play football at Iowa State?

A. Jack Trice.

Q. What community hosts the Croatian Fest?

A. Centerville.

Q. The Duesenberg brothers, who later created the automobile that bore their name, operated what kind of shop in Garner?

A. Bicycle.

◆

Q. What is the number one tourist attraction in Iowa?

A. Amana Colonies.

◆

Q. What high school team has won seventeen team state wrestling titles, the most by any school?

A. Waterloo West.

◆

Q. Where is the International Wrestling Institute and Museum located?

A. Newton.

◆

Q. What was the nickname of Gen. Francis Marion, a Revolutionary War hero honored by an annual festival in Marion, the town named after him?

A. The Swamp Fox.

◆

Q. What is the cost of a one-year fishing license?

A. $13.50.

◆

Q. The National Baseball Hall of Fame designated what Iowa-born player "the Greatest Living Right-handed Pitcher"?

A. Bob Feller (b. 1918 near Van Meter).

Q. What museum near Oskaloosa features a Quaker meeting-house and a mule cemetery?

A. Nelson Homestead Pioneer Farm and Museum.

———◆———

Q. At what Iowa college did the NFL's George Allen coach?

A. Morningside.

———◆———

Q. What Iowa event known as America's Athletic Classic is held at a university in Des Moines each April?

A. Drake Relays (first held in 1910).

———◆———

Q. What Des Moines attorney served as president of the U.S. Olympic committee?

A. Robert Helmick.

———◆———

Q. What fair is acclaimed "the World's Greatest County Fair"?

A. Clay County Fair.

———◆———

Q. Gravity High School graduate Bob King coached Larry Bird at what university?

A. Indiana State University.

———◆———

Q. What was the original nickname of the Newton High School Cardinals?

A. Little Washers.

Q. In 1990 what team did the University of Northern Iowa defeat in its only appearance in the NCAA Men's Basketball Tournament?

A. Missouri.

Q. Where is the world's only museum dedicated to preserving the history of sprint car racing?

A. Knoxville.

Q. Who was the first woman drafted by the NBA?

A. Denise Long (Union-Whitten High School, 1968).

Q. Prof. Frank D. Paine chose the name *VEISHEA* in 1922 for the Iowa State University celebration by using the first letters of what five divisions of the college?

A. Veterinary, Engineering, Industrial Science, Home Economics, and Agriculture.

Q. In the early 1970s what ballplayer from Sioux City won three World Series rings playing for the Oakland A's?

A. Dick Green.

Q. What Iowa State swimmer was a nine-time All-American and holds ten individual conference records?

A. Roger Watts.

Q. Where does historical Jesse James Day take place in June?

A. Corydon.

Q. Triplets Karen, Katie, and Kim Mazza competed in what sport for Iowa State?

A. Gymnastics.

◆

Q. Who is the winningest coach in the Cyclones' basketball history?

A. Johnny Orr.

◆

Q. How many Iowa high school wrestlers have each won four individual state championships?

A. Eleven (Maquoketa's Eric Juergens, in 1996, was the most recent).

◆

Q. Where does a Civil War reenactment of the Battle of Pea Ridge take place?

A. Keokuk.

◆

Q. Who did Frances Clarke, daughter of Gov. George W. Clarke (1913–17) marry?

A. Nile Kinnick.

◆

Q. In 1995, the boys and girls basketball teams from what high school won the state championship?

A. Winfield-Mount Union.

◆

Q. In 1968 Union Whitten High School's Denise Long repeated what 1952 feat of Monona's Norma Schulte?

A. Scoring 111 points in a basketball game.

Q. Rocky Marciano, the only undefeated boxing champion, was killed in a plane crash in what town?

A. Newton (August 31, 1969).

Q. What Hawkeye football player holds the school record with most points scored at 290?

A. Rob Houghtlin.

Q. Doreen Wilbur of Jefferson won a 1972 Olympic gold medal in what sport?

A. Archery.

Q. What is the nickname of the athletic team from Mount Saint Clare College in Clinton?

A. Mounties.

Q. What is the state's oldest and largest student-organized festival?

A. VEISHEA (since 1922).

Q. Dick Sparrow of Zearing drove how many horses in a single hitch?

A. Forty-eight (during the 1970s).

Q. What is the only organization in the nation solely devoted to interscholastic competition for girls?

A. The Iowa Girls High School Athletic Union (IGHSAU).

Q. Where was the first state fair held in 1854?

A. Fairfield (admission was 25¢).

———◆———

Q. What 1969 Guthrie Center High School graduate played football for Iowa State University and then for the Buffalo Bills?

A. Merv Krakau.

———◆———

Q. In what year was college football star Nile Kinnick named the top male athlete of the year ahead of Joe DiMaggio and Joe Louis?

A. 1939.

———◆———

Q. What is the name of the annual celebration that Atlantic began in 1992?

A. Coca-Cola Days (held the fourth weekend in September).

———◆———

Q. What was unique about the uniform tops worn by the West Point Marquette High School volleyball team in 1996?

A. They were tie-dyed (they won the Class 1-A State Championship that year).

———◆———

Q. A total of 35,072 Iowans set a world's record by consuming 20,130 pounds of what food in five hours on June 21, 1988?

A. Pork barbecue.

———◆———

Q. What European country's heritage is celebrated at annual spring festivals in Pella and Orange City?

A. Holland.

Q. Bruce Jenner, the 1976 Olympic decathlon champion, is a 1972 alumnus of what college?

A. Graceland.

Q. What professional baseball player and evangelist was born in a log cabin near Nevada?

A. Billy Sunday.

Q. Operated by Charles W. Williams just west of Independence, Rush Park featured what sport?

A. Horse racing.

Q. When Iowa State defeated Kansas in a basketball game in 1957, what Iowa State player outscored Wilt Chamberlain?

A. Gary Thompson.

Q. At the National Skillet Throw contest in Macksburg, what do the contestants try to do?

A. Knock the head off a dummy.

Q. What is the hometown of Buck Shaw, coach of the 1960 NFL-champion Philadelphia Eagles?

A. Stuart.

Q. How many downhill ski areas are in the state?

A. Seven (Sundown Mountain, Riverside Hills Area, Fun Valley, Mt. Crescent, Nor-Ski, Seven Oaks Rec., Sleepy Hollow Sports Park).

Q. In what year did Drake nearly upset UCLA and Lew Alcindor in the NCAA basketball semifinals?

A. 1969.

Q. What is the nickname of the University of Okoboji's athletic teams?

A. Fighting Phantoms.

Q. Who were Iowa State's only two wrestling coaches between 1924 and 1985?

A. Hugo Otopalik and Harold Nichols.

Q. Who is the only Iowa State All-American golfer to play on the LPGA tour since 1983?

A. Barb Thomas.

Q. What war hero won a ten-thousand-dollar, three-hundred-mile auto race in Sioux City in 1913 while wearing a bat's heart tied to his middle finger for good luck?

A. Eddie Rickenbacker.

Q. The Olson-Linn Museum in Villisca has Iowa's largest collection of what items?

A. Pre-1930s cars and trucks.

Q. University of Iowa quarterback Chuck Long finished second to whom in the 1985 Heisman Trophy race?

A. Bo Jackson.

Q. What happens at noon each second-to-last Sunday from May through September at the Field of Dreams in Dyersville?

A. The "ghost" players appear.

Q. What Bancroft native pitched for the Brooklyn Dodgers against the New York Yankees in the 1947 World Series?

A. Joe "Lefty" Hatten.

Q. In what sport has the University of Iowa won nine consecutive NCAA championships?

A. Wrestling.

Q. What is the last name of brothers Jay and Joel who played football at the University of Iowa and in the NFL?

A. Hilgenberg.

Q. What is the record for the most state football championships since a playoff system was adopted in 1972?

A. Seven (Harlan).

Q. How many no-hit baseball games did Iowa native Bob Feller pitch in the majors?

A. Three (the first in the twentieth century).

Q. How much profit was made by the first Iowa State Fair, which encouraged the Iowa Agricultural Society to make it an annual event?

A. Fifty dollars.

Q. During the late 1800s, descendants of well-to-do English families played what sport in Le Mars?

A. Polo.

◆

Q. Who was Iowa State's first Olympic wrestling champion?

A. Glenn Brand, in 1948.

◆

Q. What is known as Iowa's Antique City?

A. Walnut.

◆

Q. Lake Ellis in Lucas County has the state record for the largest flathead catfish caught, measuring fifty-two inches long and weighing how much?

A. Eighty-one pounds.

◆

Q. What town hosts the annual John L. Lewis Festival each Labor Day weekend?

A. Lucas.

◆

Q. With 2,033 points, who is the University of Northern Iowa's all-time leading scorer in basketball?

A. Jason Reese.

◆

Q. How many Big Ten titles and Rose Bowl appearances did the Hawkeyes earn under football coach Hayden Fry?

A. Three, in 1982, 1986, and 1990.

Q. What is Iowa's newest and largest recreational facility and equestrian campground and trail system?

A. Brushy Creek (Webster County).

Q. A pro baseball scout discovered the talent of Bill Zuber when he saw the teenager throw what vegetable over the roof of a barn?

A. An onion.

Q. What seven major league baseball teams have Des Moines' minor league teams been affiliated with since the 1930s?

A. St. Louis Browns, Philadelphia Phillies, L.A. Dodgers, Chicago White Sox, Oakland A's, Houston Astros, and Chicago Cubs.

Q. What town celebrates 'Hoo Doo Days' every year?

A. Neola (on Labor Day weekend).

Q. What Northern Iowa wrestler went undefeated and was a 1952 Olympic champion?

A. Bill Smith.

Q. Who in 1987 became the nation's all-time top scorer in girls' high school basketball history with 6,736 points at Ventura High School?

A. Lynne Lorenzen.

Q. What Iowan pitched and won the longest game in American League history—twenty-four innings?

A. "Iron Man" Jack Coombs.

Q. To what does *pufferbilly* of the annual Pufferbilly Days celebration in Boone refer?

A. A steam locomotive.

———◆———

Q. Who became the oldest winner of the decathlon title at the U.S. Outdoor National Track Championships on June 22, 2001?

A. Kip Janvrin (thirty-five years old).

———◆———

Q. What town hosts the National Cattle Congress?

A. Waterloo.

———◆———

Q. Lori La Deane Adams set the world record for throwing what item 175 feet, 5 inches at the Iowa Star Fair on August 21, 1979?

A. A two-pound rolling pin.

———◆———

Q. What is the last high school football team to go undefeated, untied, and unscored upon in one season?

A. Carson-Macedonia in 1973.

———◆———

Q. What Davenport native won the 1947 Heisman Trophy at Notre Dame?

A. Johnny Lujack.

———◆———

Q. What town is called "the Pumpkin Capital of Iowa" because of its Pumpkin Fest and Weigh-Off held the first Saturday of each October?

A. Anamosa.

Q. Who is the University of Iowa's all-time leading scorer in basketball with 2,116 points?

A. Roy Marble.

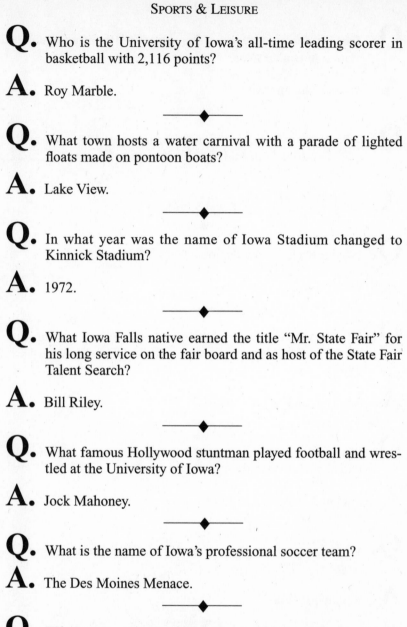

Q. What town hosts a water carnival with a parade of lighted floats made on pontoon boats?

A. Lake View.

Q. In what year was the name of Iowa Stadium changed to Kinnick Stadium?

A. 1972.

Q. What Iowa Falls native earned the title "Mr. State Fair" for his long service on the fair board and as host of the State Fair Talent Search?

A. Bill Riley.

Q. What famous Hollywood stuntman played football and wrestled at the University of Iowa?

A. Jock Mahoney.

Q. What is the name of Iowa's professional soccer team?

A. The Des Moines Menace.

Q. What was unique about the uniform worn by Drake University runner Mark Manchester when he ran the mile leg of the medley relay in the 1926 Drake Relays?

A. No pants (He forgot them and wore only his jersey, jockey strap and shoes).

Q. What Hawkeye wrestler holds the record for career pins at seventy-three and won an Olympic gold medal in 1984?

A. Ed Banach.

Q. Who broke Dan Gable's ISU wrestling record of 116 straight wins?

A. Carl Sanderson (119).

Q. What Norway native set the major-league rookie record of 374 total bases when he played for Cleveland in 1934?

A. Hal Trosky.

Q. The *George M. Verity* steamboat was given to what city in 1961 for use as a river museum?

A. Keokuk.

Q. A football victory against Northwestern (Chicago) in what year earned Iowa State its Cyclones nickname?

A. 1895.

Q. What town hosts Nordic Fest in July?

A. Decorah.

Q. What swimmer, born in Iowa City in 1962, won four medals at the 1984 Los Angeles Olympics, including two golds?

A. Nancy Hogshead.

Q. What sport did John Wayne's father play at Iowa State University and Simpson College?

A. Football.

Q. What major league baseball pitcher from Norway threw a three-hit shutout for the Baltimore Orioles in the 1983 World Series?

A. Mike Boddicker.

Q. What Bedford native set world records in the 100-yard dash and 220-yard dash in 1895?

A. John Crum.

Q. Who is the only athlete to win one hundred matches as both a collegiate wrestler and collegiate coach?

A. Dan Gable.

Q. What Holstein native was featured in *Ripley's Believe It or Not!* for having scored 279 points in nine high school football games?

A. Lester "Jack" Eicherly.

Q. What Iowa company is the sponsor of the Women's Senior Golf Classic held at Hyperion Field Club?

A. Hy-Vee.

Q. A record 252,800 fans attended what Iowa sporting event?

A. The 1999 U.S. Senior Open.

Q. What was the largest fish caught on record in Iowa?

A. A 107-pound, 69.5-inch paddle fish caught by Robert Pranschke of Onawa.

◆

Q. Who has won the most games as a Hawkeye basketball coach?

A. Tom Davis.

◆

Q. In what year was Des Moines the site of the first professional baseball game to be played at night under permanent lights?

A. 1930.

◆

Q. What school has won the most Iowa high school boys basketball state championships?

A. Davenport-Central, with nine.

◆

Q. Who set the Cyclones' single-season football record for rushing yards in a season with 2,185 in 1996?

A. Troy Davis.

◆

Q. What multiple-gold-medal-winning Olympian was the first woman to be featured as a Drake Relays contestant in 1961?

A. Wilma Rudolph.

◆

Q. What is the name of Manning's annual German heritage children's festival held on Father's Day weekend?

A. Kinderfest.

Q. "The Mayor" was the nickname of what Iowa State basketball player?

A. Fred Hoiberg.

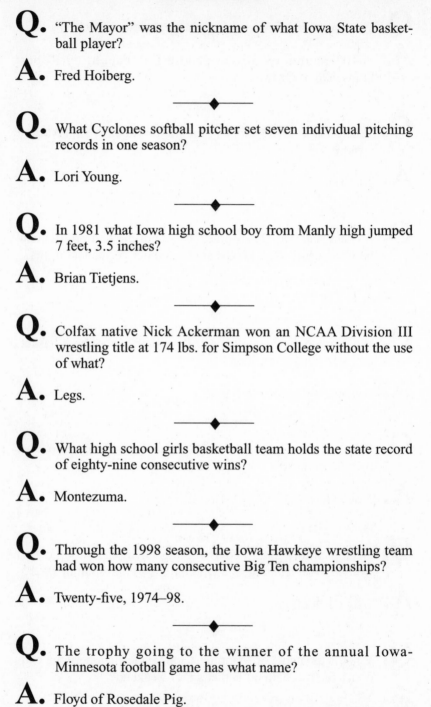

Q. What Cyclones softball pitcher set seven individual pitching records in one season?

A. Lori Young.

Q. In 1981 what Iowa high school boy from Manly high jumped 7 feet, 3.5 inches?

A. Brian Tietjens.

Q. Colfax native Nick Ackerman won an NCAA Division III wrestling title at 174 lbs. for Simpson College without the use of what?

A. Legs.

Q. What high school girls basketball team holds the state record of eighty-nine consecutive wins?

A. Montezuma.

Q. Through the 1998 season, the Iowa Hawkeye wrestling team had won how many consecutive Big Ten championships?

A. Twenty-five, 1974–98.

Q. The trophy going to the winner of the annual Iowa-Minnesota football game has what name?

A. Floyd of Rosedale Pig.

Q. In what year did Michigan State beat Iowa State in the "elite eight" NCAA men's basketball tournament?

A. 2000.

Q. In what year did the Panthers play their first football game in the University of Northern Iowa dome?

A. 1976.

Q. Who was the winner of the 1999 U.S. Senior Open held at Des Moines Golf and Country Club?

A. Dave Eichelberger.

Q. What future NFL star running back fumbled four times in the first half of the University of Iowa's 1986 Rose Bowl loss to UCLA?

A. Ronnie Harmon.

Q. Iowa State University quit playing what sport in 2001 after a 109-year history?

A. Baseball (108 seasons; none in 1897).

Q. After a disastrous fire in Spencer on June 27, 1931, what did the Iowa legislature ban?

A. Use of fireworks.

Q. Who was the only Heisman Trophy winner to play football at an Iowa college?

A. Nile Kinnick (University of Iowa, 1939).

Q. In 2000 the State of Iowa issued approximately 220,000 permits for what?

A. Boats.

Q. What year was the first Women's Senior Golf Tournament held at Hyperion Field Club in Johnston?

A. 2000.

Q. Who was Iowa State's first full-time football coach?

A. Clyde Williams.

Q. After Iowa and Iowa State stopped playing one another in football in 1934, how long was it before they renewed the rivalry?

A. Forty-three years.

Q. The inaugural 2001 Allianz Championship, a Senior PGA Tour event, was played at what country club?

A. Glen Oaks (West Des Moines).

Q. What basketball player for Mount Mercy College in Cedar Rapids from 1972 to 1976 was the first woman in Iowa college history to score one thousand points for the same school in a career?

A. Becky Steele.

Q. What Winterset-born Baseball Hall of Famer coached and played for the Pittsburgh Pirates in the first World Series in 1903?

A. Fred "Cap" Clarke.

Q. What is the highest finish of any Iowa team in the NCAA basketball tournament?

A. Second (University of Iowa, 1956).

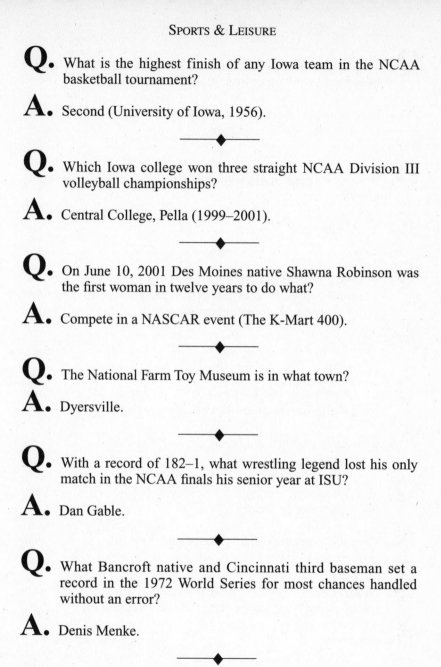

Q. Which Iowa college won three straight NCAA Division III volleyball championships?

A. Central College, Pella (1999–2001).

Q. On June 10, 2001 Des Moines native Shawna Robinson was the first woman in twelve years to do what?

A. Compete in a NASCAR event (The K-Mart 400).

Q. The National Farm Toy Museum is in what town?

A. Dyersville.

Q. With a record of 182–1, what wrestling legend lost his only match in the NCAA finals his senior year at ISU?

A. Dan Gable.

Q. What Bancroft native and Cincinnati third baseman set a record in the 1972 World Series for most chances handled without an error?

A. Denis Menke.

Q. What community hosts the annual TivoliFest in honor of its Old World heritage?

A. Elk Horn (Danish).

Q. What happened in Lake Mills on June 5, 1999, that has never happened in any other high school baseball game?

A. Four consecutive home runs (Mike Rosen, Kyle Hebrink, Bob Rogstad, and Dan Baggett).

———◆———

Q. Who was grand marshal of the VEISHEA centennial parade of 1958?

A. Ronald Reagan.

———◆———

Q. Because the town is a high point on the Illinois Central Railroad between the Missouri and Mississippi Rivers, what is the name of Alta's annual celebration?

A. Altatude Days.

———◆———

Q. St. Louis Rams' Super Bowl XXX champion MVP quarterback Kurt Warner attended what Iowa college?

A. University of Northern Iowa.

———◆———

Q. What two Iowa collegiate wrestlers were co-winners of the 2001 Dan Hodge Trophy?

A. Nick Ackerman and Cael Sanderson.

———◆———

Q. Sioux City's Sergeant Floyd Welcome Center is the only interstate highway travel center in what kind of structure?

A. Riverboat.

———◆———

Q. E. J. Runyan from Johnston set state high shcool records in how many wheel chair track and field events in 2001?

A. Four (discus, 100, 200, and 800 meter runs).

Q. In 1920, what town's high school won the state's first high school girls basketball championship?

A. Correctionville (beat Nevada 11–4).

◆

Q. While playing football at the University of Chicago, what Iowan became the first Heisman Trophy winner?

A. Jay Berwanger, in 1935.

◆

Q. Who was the last Iowa State basketball coach to lead the Cyclones to a Big Eight regular season championship and to the Final Four in the NCAA tournament?

A. Louis Menze.

◆

Q. Where is the Midwest Old Threshers Museum?

A. Mount Pleasant (farm machinery museum).

◆

Q. In 1999, Kurt Warner of Cedar Rapids became the only Iowan to receive what award?

A. NFL's MVP.

◆

Q. What is the name of a 1913 Model 30-60 Hart-Parr tractor in the Floyd County Historical Society Museum?

A. Old Reliable.

◆

Q. For what sport did Fairfield's John E. Jackson win a gold medal at the 1912 Olympics?

A. Archery.

Q. From what college wrestler did Dan Gable ask an autograph?

A. Nick Ackerman.

———◆———

Q. How many total miles were ridden across the United States during the Iowa 150 Bike Ride/A Sesquicentennial Expedition?

A. 5,047.

———◆———

Q. Iowa State has never played football against the academy of which branch of the armed services?

A. Navy.

———◆———

Q. What Iowa native and Baseball Hall of Famer was the first major league player to get three thousand base hits in a career?

A. Cap Anson.

———◆———

Q. A $10,000 investment in 1966 in what company was worth nearly $2 million in stock two years later?

A. Winnebago Company.

———◆———

Q. What Grandview College basketball player started the head-band craze in the NBA?

A. Slick Watts (with Seattle Supersonics).

———◆———

Q. What kind of fish is most frequently caught in Iowa?

A. Bluegill.

Q. Where was the first golf course west of the Mississippi constructed?

A. Fairfield.

———————◆———————

Q. How many Iowa State University wrestlers won medals at the 1972 Munich Olympics?

A. Three (Dan Gable, Ben Peterson, and Chris Taylor).

———————◆———————

Q. In what year was Jack Trice killed during a football game against Minnesota?

A. 1923.

———————◆———————

Q. As the center fielder for the Chicago White Stockings, Billy Sunday was the first man in baseball to circle the bases in as few as how many seconds?

A. Fourteen.

———————◆———————

Q. What former Dowling High School wrestling coach has the best winning percentage in dual meet victories?

A. Bob Darrah (over 95 percent, 340–17).

———————◆———————

Q. What 2000 ISU football team achievment was the first in Iowa State history?

A. A post-season bowl win (37–29 win over Pittsburg in the Insight.com Bowl).

———————◆———————

Q. Charley Williams of Independence was the only man to develop two horses to hold what record?

A. World stallion trotting record.

Q. What Davenport native was a member of Notre Dame's Four Horsemen?

A. Elmer Layden.

———◆———

Q. What Dubuque native was the bullpen ace for the St. Louis Cardinals in the 1967–68 World Series?

A. Joe Hoerner.

———◆———

Q. In what year did Dan Gable become the first American to win Olympic gold in wrestling without surrendering a single point?

A. 1972.

———◆———

Q. What Waterloo native was an outstanding punter for the University of Iowa and the Miami Dolphins?

A. Reggie Roby.

———◆———

Q. What former University of Iowa basketball player was named the NBA's 1983 Coach of the Year?

A. Don Nelson (then with the Milwaukee Bucks).

———◆———

Q. What actor, who grew up in Waterloo, was an All-Pro defensive tackle with the Detroit Lions?

A. Alex Karras.

———◆———

Q. What town hosts the National Hobo Convention?

A. Britt.

Q. What town is home to the Mesquakie Indian Powwow in August?

A. Tama.

Q. What did Dowling's 2000 football team accomplish that seven previous teams were unable to do?

A. Win the State Championship.

Q. In what year did the UI women's field hockey team win the NCAA championship?

A. 1986 (first women's national title for U of I).

Q. What town holds a Great River Days Festival featuring a Venetian boat parade and a turtle race?

A. Muscatine.

Q. How many high school girls softball championships has Ankeny won?

A. Twelve.

Q. While a player for the Chicago White Stockings, what method of batting did Billy Sunday invent?

A. Bunting.

Q. What Iowa college was the first to play in a football bowl game?

A. Drake University (Raisin Bowl, 1946).

Q. As of 2001, how many NCAA team wrestling titles had Iowa State University and University of Iowa won?

A. Twenty-seven (ISU-7, UI-20).

Q. What girls high school softball team holds the record of sixty-eight consecutive wins?

A. Urbandale (from fall '76 to spring '77).

Q. The mushroom is honored at what Cedar Rapids springtime festival?

A. Houby Days.

Q. What town has an annual Rose Festival?

A. State Center.

Q. What village celebrates National Luxembourg Day?

A. Saint Donatus.

Q. Home of the annual Sprint Car Nationals, what city has the world's fastest half-mile dirt track?

A. Knoxville.

Q. Where can one find the '93 Flood Museum?

A. Fort Madison.

Q. On the first Sunday of August each year, where is the annual Wedding Reunion held?

A. The Little Brown Church.

Q. What town hosts an annual Trek Fest the last Friday and Saturday of June?

A. Riverside.

Q. At what Iowa college did Lake Mills native and All-American defensive tackle Mike Stensrud play football before moving to the NFL?

A. Iowa State.

Q. University of Iowa swimming coach David A. Armbruster originated what swimming stroke in 1935?

A. Butterfly.

Q. The Eugene Closson Physical Education Center at Graceland College resembles what conveyance?

A. A covered wagon.

Q. What North Scott girls softball player batted .632 her senior year?

A. Lea Twigg (1993).

Q. What Orient-born Baseball Hall of Fame pitcher led his league in strikeouts for a record seven consecutive seasons?

A. Dazzy Vance.

Q. Where is the largest draft horse hitch show in North America held, featuring sixteen six-horse draft hitches?

A. Britt.

———◆———

Q. What was the last year that Iowa high school girls played six-player basketball?

A. 1993.

———◆———

Q. How did Des Moines' first Triple-A baseball team, the Iowa Oaks, get their name?

A. Named for the state tree.

———◆———

Q. How did Iowa State University students set a new Guinness Book world record on April 21, 2001?

A. For building a 2,480-pound Rice Krispie treat.

———◆———

Q. What town celebrates Frank Gotch Day every summer?

A. Humboldt.

———◆———

Q. What Cascade-born Baseball Hall of Famer was the last Chicago White Sox pitcher to win twenty-five games in a season?

A. Red Faber.

———◆———

Q. What high school holds the most girls state basketball championships with five (3 six-man & 2 five-man)?

A. Ankeny (1978, 1980, 1989, 1997, and 1999).

Q. Davenport Central High School's Roger Craig was a star running back for what NFL team most of his career?

A. The San Francisco 49ers.

Q. What town is host to the annual Tri-State Rodeo?

A. Fort Madison.

Q. Nicknamed "the Roland Rocket," who was the first two-sport All-American at Iowa State?

A. Gary Thompson (basketball and baseball).

Q. Iowa State All-American Matt Blair was drafted by what NFL team?

A. Minnesota Vikings.

Q. In 1896 the first five-player basketball game west of the Mississippi was held at what school?

A. University of Iowa.

Q. Since football playoffs began in 1972, what high school through 2000 had the best playoff winning percentage, 82.1 percent, with 55 wins and 12 losses?

A. Harlan.

Q. Who are the only two football players to have had their numbers retired by the University of Iowa?

A. Nile Kinnick (24) and Cal Jones (62).

Q. What museum near Okoboji features restored boats?

A. Iowa Great Lakes Maritime Museum.

———◆———

Q. Who was the Waterloo native that, as a rookie in 1961, gained 815 yards for the Dallas Cowboys and was selected to play in the Pro Bowl?

A. Don Perkins.

———◆———

Q. What Scranton native and former Northern Iowa player was named the NFL's 1995 defensive player of the year as a linebacker for the Buffalo Bills?

A. Bryce Paup.

———◆———

Q. Where is the Iowa Championship Rodeo held?

A. Sidney (since 1923).

———◆———

Q. What college won the Women's Softball College World Series in 1977?

A. University of Northern Iowa.

———◆———

Q. What twins were NCAA champions at the University of Iowa and Olympic medallists in 1996?

A. Terry (bronze) and Tom (gold) Brands (from Sheldon).

———◆———

Q. How many states have more golf courses per capita than Iowa?

A. None.

SCIENCE & NATURE

C H A P T E R S I X

Q. What town is famous for its cereal mills?

A. Cedar Rapids.

———◆———

Q. What type of trees were planted on the grounds of the U.S. Capitol on June 12, 1952, in memory of the five Sullivan brothers who died in 1942 during an attack on the USS *Juneau* in the Solomon Islands?

A. Crab apple.

———◆———

Q. Farmer and blacksmith John Froelich of Clayton County invented what farm implement in 1892?

A. Gas-powered tractor.

———◆———

Q. What did Des Moines' Sam Blanc invent in 1935?

A. Roto-rooter.

———◆———

Q. When did Iowa become the U.S. leader in corn production?

A. 1890.

Q. At what school did George Washington Carver receive a bachelor's degree in science?

A. Iowa State Agricultural College and Model Farm (now Iowa State University of Science and Technology).

Q. Iowa ranked first nationally in the production of what two crops in 1900?

A. Corn and oats.

Q. What city at one time had seven plants for manufacturing clayware and thus was considered the brick and tile capital of the world?

A. Mason City.

Q. What is the Iowa record amount of snowfall for one day?

A. Twenty-four inches, April 20, 1918, in Lenox.

Q. What term was used to describe the resistance of farmers to the testing of dairy cattle by state veterinarians in 1931?

A. Cow War.

Q. How many different types of fish are found in Iowa?

A. 149.

Q. Early settlers discovered what type of animal bones in a narrow ravine called Boneyard Hollow, now part of Dolliver State Park?

A. Buffalo.

Q. What underground river cavern is near McGregor?

A. Spook Cave.

———◆———

Q. How many tornadoes does Iowa average a year?

A. Thirty-four.

———◆———

Q. In 1895 what health-care therapy originated in Davenport?

A. Chiropractic.

———◆———

Q. Where did Fred Dusenberg and Edward R. Mason drive their car in order to demonstrate its ability to climb hills?

A. Up the west steps of the state capitol.

———◆———

Q. Situated in Dubuque, what is the world's steepest and shortest railway?

A. Fenelon Place Elevator.

———◆———

Q. What was the first car to have four-wheel hydraulic brakes?

A. Duesenberg Model A.

———◆———

Q. Graduating seniors and faculty members of Wartburg College plant what flowers on campus after each spring's baccalaureate service?

A. Marigolds.

Q. Where was the first gasoline traction engine made?

A. Froelich.

———◆———

Q. Where was the first light bulb in the state, purchased for a mine in Cleveland, Iowa, actually turned on?

A. Lucas.

———◆———

Q. Astronauts David C. Hilmers, George "Pinky" Nelson, and Dale Garner were all residents of what county?

A. Clinton.

———◆———

Q. In 2000 what was the value of the average farm acre?

A. $1,857.

———◆———

Q. William "Shorty" Paul, team physician for the Iowa Hawkeyes until his death in 1977, was recognized as the developer of what two pharmaceutical products?

A. Bufferin & Rolaids.

———◆———

Q. Mineral water from what town was sent in barrels to the White House by order of President Grover Cleveland's physician?

A. Colfax.

———◆———

Q. What Iowa State University professor is considered the father of the electronic digital computer?

A. John Vincent Atanasoff.

Q. In 1938 the Adams Ranch in Sac County was the largest single block of farmland in the state with how many acres?

A. More than seven thousand.

———◆———

Q. Who invented a flying machine similar to a helicopter in Imogene in 1886?

A. August Werner.

———◆———

Q. Where was the first reinforced concrete arch bridge in the U.S. built?

A. Across Dry Creek in Lyon County (1893).

———◆———

Q. Motor Mill, southeast of Elkader and the tallest mill in the Midwest, is constructed of what material?

A. Native limestone.

———◆———

Q. Honoring Iowa soldiers from the Civil War to the present, where is the Gold Star Museum?

A. Camp Dodge (Johnston).

———◆———

Q. A children's hospital was added to the University of Iowa Hospitals in what year?

A. 1919.

———◆———

Q. What type of road was built between Mount Pleasant and Burlington in the mid-1800s?

A. Plank.

Q. Muscatine Island is most noted for what fruit?

A. Watermelon.

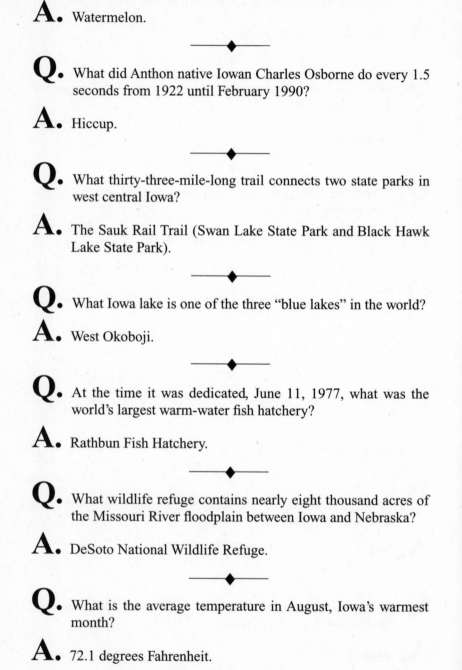

Q. What did Anthon native Iowan Charles Osborne do every 1.5 seconds from 1922 until February 1990?

A. Hiccup.

Q. What thirty-three-mile-long trail connects two state parks in west central Iowa?

A. The Sauk Rail Trail (Swan Lake State Park and Black Hawk Lake State Park).

Q. What Iowa lake is one of the three "blue lakes" in the world?

A. West Okoboji.

Q. At the time it was dedicated, June 11, 1977, what was the world's largest warm-water fish hatchery?

A. Rathbun Fish Hatchery.

Q. What wildlife refuge contains nearly eight thousand acres of the Missouri River floodplain between Iowa and Nebraska?

A. DeSoto National Wildlife Refuge.

Q. What is the average temperature in August, Iowa's warmest month?

A. 72.1 degrees Fahrenheit.

Q. Who made the first recorded airplane flight in Iowa on May 10, 1910?

A. Arthur J. Hartman.

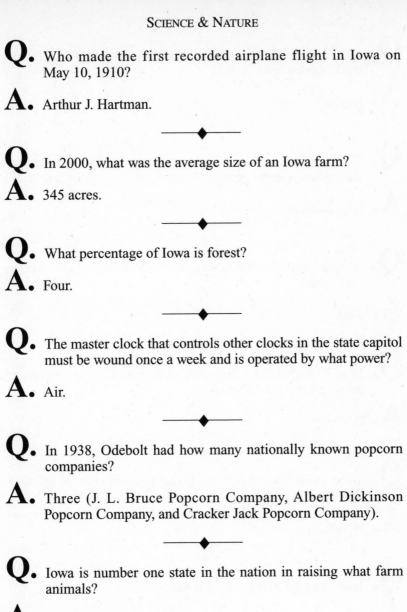

Q. In 2000, what was the average size of an Iowa farm?

A. 345 acres.

Q. What percentage of Iowa is forest?

A. Four.

Q. The master clock that controls other clocks in the state capitol must be wound once a week and is operated by what power?

A. Air.

Q. In 1938, Odebolt had how many nationally known popcorn companies?

A. Three (J. L. Bruce Popcorn Company, Albert Dickinson Popcorn Company, and Cracker Jack Popcorn Company).

Q. Iowa is number one state in the nation in raising what farm animals?

A. Hogs (24 percent of total).

Q. New Virginia claims to be the birthplace of what breed of cattle in 1902?

A. Polled Hereford.

Q. Fort Dodge is one of the world's leading makers of products made from what mineral?

A. Gypsum.

———◆———

Q. During the Civil War, Keokuk's Annie Wittenmyer was instrumental in establishing what facilities in army hospitals?

A. Diet kitchens.

———◆———

Q. In what year did the Quaker Oats Company begin making Life cereal?

A. 1958.

———◆———

Q. In 1879 Kalona had a shorthorn breeding service that earned what nickname for the town?

A. Bulltown.

———◆———

Q. What Iowa county has the highest percentage of grade-A topsoil in the nation?

A. Wright.

———◆———

Q. Iowa has how many state forests?

A. Nine.

———◆———

Q. What 1935 Iowa State alumnus developed the first single-cross hybrid corn for volume production?

A. Raymond Baker.

Q. In 1891 a large glacial boulder found in Black Hawk County was used to construct what building in Waterloo?

A. Boulder Church.

———◆———

Q. What state park contains thirteen limestone caves and a natural bridge?

A. Maquoketa.

———◆———

Q. Who designed the first flexible door hanger and monorail conveyor system in 1919 in Fairfield?

A. William Louden.

———◆———

Q. Where is the production center of Hy-Line International, the world's largest producer of breeding stock for egg-laying chickens?

A. Dallas Center.

———◆———

Q. What was the first man-made lake in Iowa?

A. Pine Lake.

———◆———

Q. How much of Iowa's land was given to railroad companies?

A. About 10 percent.

———◆———

Q. Born in Des Moines in 1877, who invented the electric razor?

A. Jacob Schick.

Q. What is considered the greatest natural disaster in Iowa's history?

A. The flood of 1993.

Q. What is the average annual rainfall in Iowa?

A. Thirty-two inches.

Q. What percentage of the nation's corn is grown in Iowa?

A. Eighteen.

Q. Where is the Exploratorium of Iowa located?

A. Ottumwa.

Q. Amelia Earhart took her first flying lessons from what ex-Iowan in California?

A. Neta Snook (Ames).

Q. What is Iowa's national ranking in number of flocks of sheep?

A. Second.

Q. During the summer of 1936, Allamakee County offered a bounty of fifty cents for three inches of tail from what creatures?

A. Rattlesnakes.

Q. In what year was the Iowa Board of Veterinary Medicine created?

A. 1900.

———◆———

Q. How much do the sheets of twenty-three-carat gold on the dome of the Iowa capitol weigh?

A. One hundred ounces each.

———◆———

Q. George Gallup, the statistician who established opinion-poll-sampling techniques, was born in 1901 in what town?

A. Jefferson.

———◆———

Q. Where was the world's first academic program linking veterinary medicine and electrical engineering (called biomedical engineering) established?

A. Iowa State University.

———◆———

Q. Where is the world's largest roller dam located?

A. Davenport.

———◆———

Q. Clam shells found at the bend of a river near Muscatine led to what industry?

A. Pearl button making.

———◆———

Q. Loras College has the world's largest live collection of what algae?

A. Diatoms.

Q. In 1880 what Waterloo resident became the first president of AT&T?

A. Theodore Vail.

Q. Using the fruits, vegetables, and blossoms of rhubarb, dandelion, red clover, and cherry, what is produced in Amana?

A. Wine.

Q. A telephone museum can be found in what Iowa town?

A. Jefferson.

Q. The wreck of what 1864 steamboat can be seen at the DeSoto National Wildlife Refuge?

A. The *Bertrand*.

Q. A large bird's nest in a grove of oak trees above the Boone River gave what town its name?

A. Eagle Grove.

Q. Where does Iowa rank nationally in livestock and livestock products?

A. Second (behind only Texas).

Q. Where was the first rotary pump built?

A. Cedar Falls.

Q. In 1920 what company was established when Henry A. Wallace and his partner Jay J. Newlin began to raise hybridized seed corn to sell near Johnston?

A. Pioneer Hi-bred International, Inc.

———◆———

Q. Farmers from what county were the first to produce electricity on farmer-owned lines?

A. Franklin (March 28, 1938).

———◆———

Q. What is Iowa's average annual snowfall?

A. Thirty-two inches.

———◆———

Q. How tall was the world's tallest corn stalk, grown by Don Radda of Washington in 1946?

A. Thirty-one feet, three inches.

———◆———

Q. What is the state's record high temperature?

A. 118 degrees Fahrenheit, in Keokuk on July 20, 1934.

———◆———

Q. Born on a farm near Provitin, who was the only agriculturalist to win a Nobel Peace Prize?

A. Dr. Norman Borlaug.

———◆———

Q. On the bluffs of what river is one of only three locations in the world where cliff-dwelling pigeons can be found?

A. Iowa River.

Q. The panic of 1873, coupled with a plague of what insect, led to the closing of the mills in Milford?

A. Grasshoppers.

Q. How many acres of Iowa are farmland?

A. 32.8 million.

Q. When a dike broke after torrential rains in 1986, Crystal Lake, a thirty-five-acre lake near DeWitt, drained in how many minutes?

A. Fifteen.

Q. What county had the first tax-supported hospital in the nation?

A. Washington.

Q. What is the last name of the father and son who invented and developed chiropractic?

A. Palmer.

Q. For what invention did Dubuque's John L. Harvey receive a patent in 1856?

A. Paper clip.

Q. What percentage of Iowa land is arable?

A. 94 percent.

Q. What type of tree near Perry, rated the finest of its species by the Iowa Federated Garden Clubs in 1936, started as a fishing pole stuck in the ground?

A. Cottonwood.

———◆———

Q. What is the largest cereal factory in the world?

A. Quaker Oats.

———◆———

Q. What year saw record low yields in corn, hay, oats, rye, and soybeans?

A. 1934.

———◆———

Q. In what town did an artesian well drilled in August 1886 spout so strongly that efforts to harness it continued until October 1887?

A. Belle Plaine.

———◆———

Q. How many different varieties of ferns have been found in Wildcat Den State Park near Muscatine?

A. Twenty-five.

———◆———

Q. The average Iowa dairy cow produces how many gallons of milk a day?

A. Six (the best produce seventeen).

———◆———

Q. When was the first recorded earthquake in Iowa?

A. January 4, 1843.

Q. What national figure planted a tree in the park in Keokuk in 1903?

A. President Theodore Roosevelt.

◆

Q. What is the state rock?

A. Geode.

◆

Q. Developed at the University of Iowa, the nationally administered Iowa Test of Basic Skills was first given Iowa school children in what year?

A. 1935.

◆

Q. In 1910 what Iowan became the first person to make a ship-to-shore flight in an airplane?

A. Eugene B. Ely.

◆

Q. What Cedar Rapids physician developed x-ray treatment for cancer?

A. Arthur Erskine.

◆

Q. What University of Iowa professor developed the Iowa Test of Basic Skills, the Iowa Test of Educational Development and co-founded the ACT program?

A. E. F. Lindquist.

◆

Q. A fossil park in the open pits of a former brick and tile plant is near what town?

A. Rockford.

Q. Where is Iowa's only fire tower situated?

A. Yellow River State Forest.

———◆———

Q. Founded in 1954, Ida Grove's Midwest Industries, Inc., developed what type of equipment used in one form on farms and in another form on waterfronts?

A. Hoist.

———◆———

Q. In 2000, Iowa ranked first nationally in the production of pork, corn, and what other agri-product?

A. Eggs.

———◆———

Q. In what year did Maytag produce its last wringer washing machines?

A. 1983.

———◆———

Q. What former towns are now at the bottom of Lake Red Rock?

A. Cordova & Red Rock (and half of Swan).

———◆———

Q. Robert N. Noyce, who invented the microchip and received the National Medal of Science, was a graduate of what college?

A. Grinnell.

———◆———

Q. What was the second town west of the Mississippi to have electric lighting and was the first to have a public power system?

A. Fairfield.

Q. What is Iowa's chief fruit crop?

A. Apples.

———◆———

Q. Spirit Lake is especially noted for what type of fish?

A. Pike.

———◆———

Q. George Washington Carver taught what subject for two years at Iowa State?

A. Botany.

———◆———

Q. What is the average annual temperature in Iowa?

A. Forty-eight degrees Fahrenheit.

———◆———

Q. What is the state bird?

A. Eastern goldfinch.

———◆———

Q. What Des Moines man built the first successful electric car in the United States and demonstrated it in 1888?

A. William Morrison.

———◆———

Q. With eight women in its class, the University of Iowa's medical department became the first coeducational medical school in what year?

A. 1870.

Q. The purchase of what 240-acre state preserve by the Iowa Conservation Commission in 1945 was the beginning of the state's prairie protection efforts?

A. Hayden Prairie.

———◆———

Q. What physicist—born, educated, and employed in Iowa—in 1958 discovered the radiation belts that circle the earth, which were named for him?

A. James A. Van Allen (Van Allen radiation belts).

———◆———

Q. The University of Iowa Hospital at Iowa City was established in what year?

A. 1898.

———◆———

Q. Aside from the fur trade, what was the state's first business enterprise?

A. Lead mining.

———◆———

Q. About how many bushels of corn are grown annually in Iowa?

A. 1.75 billion (on 11.8 million acres).

———◆———

Q. What is normally the rainiest month?

A. June.

———◆———

Q. What national wildlife refuge is the watershed for both the Blue Earth and Des Moines Rivers and therefore has water that runs both north and south?

A. Union Slough in Kossuth County.

Q. Near what town is the Kate Shelley High Bridge, one of the world's highest double-track railroad bridges?

A. Boone.

———◆———

Q. For what cheese is the Maytag Dairy Farm especially noted?

A. Maytag Blue Cheese.

———◆———

Q. What company in Cedar Rapids utilizes a large share of Iowa's oat crop?

A. Quaker Oats.

———◆———

Q. What Latimer dentist invented the plastic eye and glass eye?

A. Dr. Milton Wirtz.

———◆———

Q. The Pleasant Creek Recreation Area has the most northerly strand of what kind of tree in the Western Hemisphere?

A. Pecan.

———◆———

Q. Where was the first statistical laboratory in the nation?

A. Iowa State University.

———◆———

Q. What pioneer aviator from Denison broke the long-distance record set by Lindbergh and also flew the first transatlantic mail flight in 1927?

A. Clarence D. Chamberlin.

Q. What Council Bluffs–born inventor patented the vacuum tube, basic to the development of long-distance radio and television communication?

A. Dr. Lee De Forest (1873–1961).

———◆———

Q. Who gave Pella's Formal Tulip Gardens its first twenty-five thousand bulbs?

A. The Holland Flower Bulb Growers Association.

———◆———

Q. What is the state flower?

A. Wild rose.

———◆———

Q. A rare earthquake tremor measuring between four and five on the Richter scale shook parts of eastern Iowa in what year?

A. 1972.

———◆———

Q. What corporation is the world's second largest window and door manufacturer?

A. Pella Corporation.

———◆———

Q. In what town is the Bily Clock Museum located?

A. Spillville.

———◆———

Q. Iowa's coal mining peaked in 1917 when it ranked in what spot in national production?

A. Tenth (9 million tons).

Q. How many apples did the Delicious apple tree bear during its first year of production?

A. One.

◆

Q. Iowa has had more recorded tornadoes than any other state except which one?

A. Kansas.

◆

Q. The meat-packing industry in Sioux City started by accident after a boat containing what product sank in the Missouri River?

A. Wheat.

◆

Q. What Northwood High School graduate became the president of Gulf Oil?

A. Sidney Swensrud.

◆

Q. What was the record rainfall for one day, which occurred in Larrabee in Cherokee County on June 24, 1891?

A. 12.99 inches.

◆

Q. Dr. Robert Millikan, born in Maquoketa in 1868, was the first American to win the Nobel Prize in what field?

A. Physics.

◆

Q. Where is the state's only long-range radar station located?

A. Arlington.

Q. Situated in Davenport, what was the first hospital built in Iowa?

A. Mercy Hospital.

◆

Q. Besides gravel and gypsum, what is the other nonfuel substance produced in Iowa?

A. Portland cement.

◆

Q. What is the principal poultry raised in Iowa?

A. Turkey.

◆

Q. In what year did Quaker Oats begin producing Cap'n Crunch cereal?

A. 1963.

◆

Q. What Iowa town bills itself as the home of the world's largest horse sale?

A. Waverly.

◆

Q. What Iowa State University graduate helped create the prototype for the Rice Krispie treat while employed at Kellogg's?

A. Mildred Day (ISU–Home Economics, 1928).

◆

Q. What cave near Dubuque contains formations known as anthodites or cave flowers?

A. Crystal Lake Cave.

Q. What Iowa farmer, one of the world's largest producers of hybrid seed corn, shared his knowledge of good farming methods with Russia in the midst of the Cold War?

A. Roswell Garst.

Q. Who invented the large round hay baler?

A. Gary Vermeer of Vermeer Manufacturing, Pella.

Q. Where is Iowa's only floating sphagnum bog?

A. Pilot Knob State Park in Dead Man's Lake.

Q. Dr. Lucy Hobbs, who lived in McGregor from 1862 to 1865, was the first woman to receive what degree?

A. Doctor of Dental Surgery.

Q. Estherville is the site of one of the largest meteorites on record which crashed two miles north of the city on May 10 of what year?

A. 1879.

Q. Christian K. Nelson invented what ice cream novelty?

A. Eskimo Pies.

Q. On May 15 of what year did a tornado hit Charles City, destroying 265 businesses, 1,203 homes, and 1,250 cars, and killing 13 people?

A. 1968.

Q. Situated two-and-one-half miles southwest of Strawberry Point, what is Iowa's oldest state park?

A. Backbone.

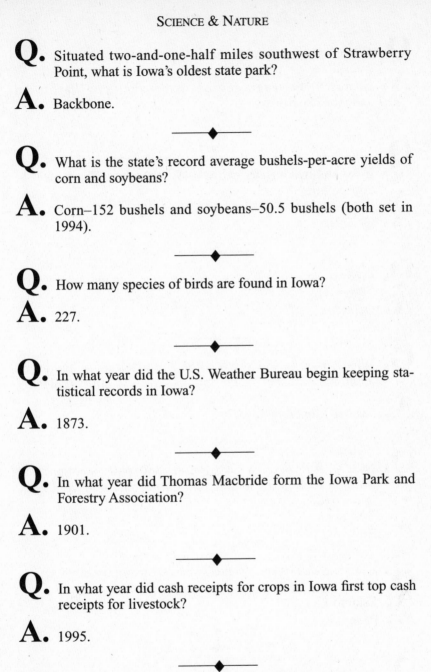

Q. What is the state's record average bushels-per-acre yields of corn and soybeans?

A. Corn–152 bushels and soybeans–50.5 bushels (both set in 1994).

Q. How many species of birds are found in Iowa?

A. 227.

Q. In what year did the U.S. Weather Bureau begin keeping statistical records in Iowa?

A. 1873.

Q. In what year did Thomas Macbride form the Iowa Park and Forestry Association?

A. 1901.

Q. In what year did cash receipts for crops in Iowa first top cash receipts for livestock?

A. 1995.

Q. What is Iowa's most valuable crop export?

A. Soybeans.

Q. What is the state's record low temperature?

A. Minus forty-seven degrees Fahrenheit, in Washta on January 12, 1912.

Q. Who was appointed the first national director of boys' and girls' club work (later called 4-H) in the U.S. Department of Agriculture?

A. O. H. Benson.

Q. What is the largest pork-producing county in the world?

A. Delaware.

Q. What company in Cresco is the nation's leading builder of aluminum livestock, horse, motorsports, and utility trailers?

A. Feather-Lite Trailers.

Q. Near what town did a surveyor, in 1880, place a cottonwood walking stick in the middle of the road only to have it grow into a tree?

A. Anita.

Q. What is the number one game bird in the state?

A. Pheasant.

Q. The disciplines of educational testing and speech pathology began at what institution?

A. University of Iowa.

Q. Situated in Muscatine, what is the largest canning plant between the Mississippi River and the Rocky Mountains?

A. H. J. Heinz Company.

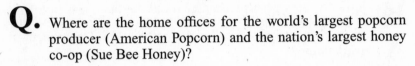

Q. Where are the home offices for the world's largest popcorn producer (American Popcorn) and the nation's largest honey co-op (Sue Bee Honey)?

A. Sioux City.

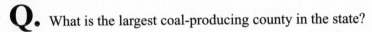

Q. In what year did a tornado kill fifteen people south of DeWitt, continuing on its path of destruction and death to Camanche?

A. 1860.

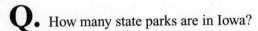

Q. What is the largest coal-producing county in the state?

A. Marion.

Q. How many state parks are in Iowa?

A. Eighty-four.

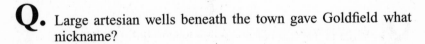

Q. Large artesian wells beneath the town gave Goldfield what nickname?

A. Fountain City.

Q. During the flood of 1993, for how many days was the entire city of Des Moines without drinking water?

A. Twenty.

Q. What is the state tree?

A. Oak.

Q. Iowa contains what percentage of all the first-class farmland in the United States?

A. 25 percent.

Q. Situated at Fort Madison, what is the name of the largest double-deck, swing-span bridge in the world?

A. Santa Fe Bridge.

Q. What two crops make up more than 94 percent of the total value of production in the state?

A. Corn and soybeans.

Q. What laboratory was established by Thomas H. Macbride for "the study of nature in nature"?

A. Iowa Lakeside Laboratory.

Q. What county has the most acreage of apple orchards?

A. Harrison.

Q. Where is the home of Wells' Dairy, best known for Blue Bunny products?

A. Le Mars.

Q. What is the only natural substance that can be restored to its original rocklike state by adding water?

A. Gypsum.

◆

Q. January, the coldest month, averages what temperature?

A. 17.3 degrees Fahrenheit.

◆

Q. What Iowa State scientist and his associates developed an economical method of extracting uranium from uranium fluoride?

A. Dr. Frank Spedding.

◆

Q. What pioneer aviators lived in Cedar Rapids for a while as children?

A. Wilbur & Orville Wright (1878–1881).

◆

Q. What ten-foot-high clock is in Spillville?

A. The American Pioneer History Clock.

◆

Q. What county has a state hatchery that raises quail and pheasants?

A. Boone.

◆

Q. When was the snowiest month recorded in Iowa history?

A. December 2000 (24.7" averaged statewide).

Q. In 1994 what Maharishi University of Management professor returned more than $600,000 in federal grant money on the ethical grounds his DNA research might lead to dangerous applications?

A. Dr. John Fagan.

◆

Q. Jesse Hiatt of Peru was the first to grow what new fruit?

A. Delicious apple.

◆

Q. Iowa State's Hilton Coliseum was flooded up to the center-court scoreboard in what year?

A. 1993.

◆

Q. What chemist invented nylon on February 28, 1935?

A. Wallace Carothers (1896–1937, from Burlington).

◆

Q. Where is the Home of Iowa's Largest Underground Limestone Mine?

A. Douds.

◆

Q. What Spencer woman is credited with using the word *blizzard* in 1868 to describe a fierce snowstorm after reading a story about a man named Mr. Blizzard who had a raging temper?

A. Lephe Wells Coates.